AF446717

The

Greater

Healing

LifeBridge Tyler Church
903-871-5120
Lifebridgetyler.com

The

Greater

Healing

The Journey from Brokenness to Joy through God's Love

Marty Sholars
with Kay Walter

The Greater Healing

Copyright ©1996 by Marty Sholars. All rights reserved. No part of this publication may be reproduced, stored in a retrieval system, or transmitted in any form or by any means — electronic, mechanical, photocopy, recording, or any other — except for brief quotations in printed reviews, without the prior permission of the author.

Scripture quotations are from the HOLY BIBLE, NEW INTERNATIONAL VERSION.
Copyright © 1973, 1978, 1984 International Bible Society. Used by permission of Zondervan
Bible Publishers.

Cover design and illustrations by Joy Schulke.

ISBN 0-9660360-1-8
Printed in the United States of America

Marty Sholars Enterprises, Publisher
P. O. Box 654
Katy, Texas 77492

To my husband, Nick, and my children, Meredith and Kent, with all my love.
I treasure each of you and thank you for the light and joy you bring to my life.

Contents

Acknowledgments

This project began several years ago as thoughts in my head, feelings in my heart, and lots of scribbled notes. But after a year of weekly meetings with my friend Denise Billings, a high school English teacher, a book began to take shape. Her commitment and diligence, along with her expertise and organizational skills, brought order and form to the material.

God brought Kay Walter into my life to continue the project by doing the arduous job of editing the material. As we worked together, her role expanded significantly as she rewrote, added to, and fleshed out chapters as God gave me fresh insights and greater understanding. With her gifted and creative talent, she was able to make my thoughts come to life on the page. It was so exciting to look at what she wrote and say, "Yes, that's what I mean!"

When I asked Joy Schulke to illustrate the text, as well as the front cover, I really had no idea of the extent of her talent. She has brought my feelings to life in color and drawings, capturing the spirit of my book through art.

My husband, Nick, supported and encouraged me since the beginning, when we spent a week at the beach so that I could start putting my thoughts on paper. My children, Meredith and Kent, have been very patient and supportive as well throughout the birthing of this book. They give me so much inspiration and hope, and are a constant reminder of God's most gracious and precious gifts.

Special thanks to my "Experiencing God" Bible Study group: Pat Kourie, Kymn Chapman, Carol Minze, Les Ann Hernandez, Karen House, Betty Pedlar, Marsha Cook, Suzanne Ball, Sharon Watson, Julie Rifley, and Millie Baldwin. These ladies inspired and encouraged me to pursue this "God-sized" task. And David and Tammy Dewhurst expressed their wholehearted belief in my work and were committed to making this book a reality.

All in all, it is a book that was compiled through the love, tears, joy, and pain of all the people I have met. My clients provide more inspiration and teaching to me than they know. I appreciate the holy privilege of being allowed to watch the healing power of Christ in each of their lives as they open themselves to His power and grace. I also recognize my many friends, who provide the warmth and kindness that enrich my life. Their laughter, tears, and shared experience have contributed to this work as well.

The connectedness and interdependence of each of us is represented by all that it took for this book to be published. With sincere gratitude, I thank you, one and all!

Preface

Ever since the Garden of Eden, humankind has been presented with a choice that overshadows and supersedes all others: to live our life God's way or to go our own way. We read the Biblical accounts of God's children following the path of fellowship and obedience for only a short time and then falling away again and again as they tried to live like everyone around them, continually breaking God's heart with their stubborn willfulness.

We smugly think to ourselves, "Why were they so dense? Hadn't God parted the Red Sea and provided manna and quail? Didn't He help them conquer their enemies? God even came to earth as a man, Jesus Christ. He performed miracles right in front of them, yet they put Him to death. Why didn't they recognize God's help when He sent it?" Yet aren't we stubborn and willful as well?

While we have the full revelation of God through Scripture, the witness of the life of Christ, and the indwelling presence of the Holy Spirit, we still try to live in our own strength. We've trusted God for the most important thing — our salvation from sin and death through the work of Christ on the cross. Yet we fail to live the abundant life that Christ promised us because we try to manage the rest of life on our own terms, oftentimes in ways that are identical to those of people who don't know our Savior. Why are _we_ so dense?

I was privileged to grow up in a loving, Christian home, where I came to know Jesus as Savior and Lord at an early age. Through the years, I recognized that Christians have a hope for the future and eternity that is foreign to nonbelievers, but I could see only a slight degree of difference in how people handled the hurts and disappointments of day-to-day life. I particularly remember the terrible anguish my family and I experienced years ago when my cousin committed suicide. How could he have been so hopeless? In the midst of that dark time, I determined that I would help people who were bruised and battered by their life experiences.

In time, an understanding of God's plan for our strength and sufficiency in Him evolved as I studied God's word and recognized the failings of many of the approaches of conventional psychology. I became a Christian counselor, teaching my clients these principles and joyously watching the healing and transformation take place as they began to walk in step with Christ and to accept His healing love. As this "theology of healing love" took shape, I began speaking before groups, but found that time constraints hampered a full presentation. The necessity of a book became apparent.

It truly grieves me that people struggle through life trying to shoulder their burdens, alleviate their suffering, bury their sorrows, and "tough it out" on their own, when God wants so much to come alongside and lead us to healing and wholeness. For this reason, I hope you will attentively read each chapter. Completing the assignments will help you get the greatest benefit from the teaching.

My prayer is that, before you reach the final page, you will recognize the sufficiency of God's love to make you whole and healthy.

Assignment
Personal Mission Statement

Before you read further in this book, take time to write your own personal mission statement on the following page. This is a statement that summarizes your personal goal as an individual — that is, what you hope to accomplish with your life. It should be worded in generalized terms so that it will last a lifetime. Keep in mind, though, that it can be added to, or modified, at any time.

A personal mission statement must include only such elements that are within your control and not those that are determined by other people. For example, your statement might include something about being a good parent to your children, but it should not be stated in terms such as "having happy, well-adjusted, successful children."

Some examples of personal mission statements are:

      a) to reflect the image of Christ

      b) to love as Christ loves me

      c) to be a servant of Christ

      d) to demonstrate the talents and abilities God has entrusted to my care

      e) to become all Christ created me to be.

The point of this exercise is twofold: First, to see if your personal mission statement is altered in any way by reading this book. Second, to determine what is blocking your ability to carry out your personal mission statement. Those blocks are probably indicators of what needs healing in your life.

Date:

Personal Mission Statement:

Chapter 1
Our Spirit

"In him we live and move and have our being." Acts 17:28

What is it that is suffering so miserably inside us that does not respond to bandages, medicine, or surgery? Why is it that despite the best advice and the strongest willpower, we continue to walk in defeat and despair? What's missing from our search for healing?

The answer to all of these question begins with a recognition that we are not just sophisticated, culturally advanced animals. When God breathed life into the man and woman He created, He gave them far more than life-sustaining oxygen. He gave them part of Himself — a spirit nature.

In order to understand the concept of spirit, we must first remember that we were created by God for fellowship with Him. The supernatural Creator of the universe wanted interaction and relationship with the flesh-and-blood mortals whom He had made. It therefore follows that He had to give us the means for fellowship with the divine as an aspect of our "being-ness."

We were also created in the image of God. (Genesis 1:27) In this case, image does not refer to our physical form but to the fact that He created us to reflect His character. If our character is to bear witness to Him, it is essential that we have a component in our own nature that allows us to experience and demonstrate God's character.

Spirit, then, cannot be defined in terms apart from God. In fact, our spirit is best described in God-relational terms, for it exists as an expression of our completion in, and oneness with, our Creator.

I believe that our spirit is shaped by five important elements:

1. God's love for us - This is the love that has been available to us since the foundation of the world. Since it is His nature to love, God cannot keep from loving us. It is the driving force behind the fellowship that He wants to have with us as well as the model for the unconditional love He calls us to give to others.

We must first remember that we were created by God for fellowship with Him.

Spirit cannot be defined in terms apart from God.

2. Our relationship with Christ - Christ is our connection point to God. Through Him and the indwelling Holy Spirit, whom we received when we professed our faith in Christ as Savior and Lord, we can experience relationship with God and reflect God's character to others. Note that the foundation of this relationship with Christ is faith. It is not based on our performance or our behavior.

3. Our worth and value in God's eyes - At the time of creation, God declared that what He had made was very good. Although we have strayed far from the garden, He still sees us as having worth and value because He looks at us through Christ's redeeming blood. The esteem of God is given to us because of His grace, love, and mercy — regardless of what we have, or have not, done. We cannot make ourselves worthy or valuable.

4. Our God-created individuality - There is great diversity among the children of God. It is as though He infused us with infinite variety in personality, talents, abilities, and spiritual gifts because He created us for fellowship and pleasure throughout eternity.

5. God's purpose for our lives - Our spirit is also shaped by the special purpose that God has for each of His children. As we put ourselves in His hands, we can trust that our unique life purpose will give us direction and energize us with passion and vitality.

It's important to back up slightly to clarify point No. 3 above. The popular concept of self-esteem refers to pride in oneself and implies a valuation based on how we feel about our efforts and whether or not we succeed or fail. If that were true, our worth and value are very conditional and circumstantial.

Fortunately for all of us, our worth and value are God- given constants in our life. Like God's love, His esteem for us remains the same. In reality, the only thing that varies is our confidence in our worth in God's eyes, and that confidence can fluctuate with our life circumstances.

If we have a talent for playing the piano — that is, the ability to play the piano comes very easily to us — our confidence in the gift will rise and fall as a function of circumstances, such as the number of hours we spend practicing the piano. Yet, the gift is present whether we practice or not. Likewise, our confidence in God's gift to us rises and falls as we experience hurt feelings, successes, failures, joys, and frustrations. But our worth and God's esteem are "set in concrete," so to speak, because they were established on the cross.

Our spiritual state
Just as we sometimes don't comprehend our worth and value in God's eyes, we may also fail to embrace His love; we allow our relationship with Christ to grow cold; and we may lose sight of our God-created individuality and

Your Spirit

Five elements
shape your spirit:

1. God's love for you

2. Your relationship
   with Christ

3. Your worth and value
   in God's eyes

4. Your God-created
   individuality

5. God's purpose
   for your life

life purpose. We also experience highs and lows triggered by a wide range of circumstances and events in our lives, as well as illness, injury, and death. All of these affect our feelings about ourselves and God, and greatly influence our choices and responses. Through this combination of external effect and internal neglect, our spiritual state suffers. This is the pain that underlies our traumas in life and continues to exist for years afterward. We will never be truly healed and whole until our spirits are healed and restored as well.

Since our spirit is the God-oriented aspect of our being, it follows that the remedy for our spiritual suffering is found only through God. Our task is to recognize our spiritual poverty apart from God and seek healing in His loving hands.

We will never be truly healed and whole until our spirits are healed and restored as well.

The remedy for our spiritual suffering is found only through God.

Chapter 2
Needs of the Spirit

"And my God will meet all your needs according

to his glorious riches in Christ Jesus."   Philippians 4:19

As noted in the previous chapter, God created us with a spirit so that we could have fellowship with Him and He with us. Just as the physical body He designed needs food, water, exercise, and rest in order to grow and flourish, our spirit has needs that must be met in order to develop and mature as God intended. When these spiritual needs are satisfied, it is possible for us to experience true intimacy with God as well as healthy relationships with others.

I have identified eight needs of the spirit: safety, security, value, acceptance, nurturing, understanding, forgiveness, and belonging.

Eight needs of the spirit

1. **Safety** - Spiritual safety give us the confidence to honestly be ourselves because we have no fear of abandonment or rejection. Christ assures us, "I am with you always, even to the end of the age." (Matthew 28:20)

   When we experience a loss or suffer neglect, or we are denied physical or emotional safety, the consequences we suffer can be far-reaching. A woman came to see me who was suffering from terrible fear and anxiety about her life, so much so that she was worried about her own death, the death of her children, disease, etc. As we began to examine her life, Cheryl recognized obvious holes in her early life. Her father was a raging alcoholic and her mother, who was in denial, provided little in the way of nurture for her. As a result, Cheryl became the caretaker in the family, effectively assuming the role of parent to her parents. In time she came to see that her present-day fear and anxiety were rooted in her childhood insecurities about her safety.

2. **Security** - Spiritual security grows out of order, stability, and consistency; whereas, disorder and lack of predictability cause

When our spiritual needs are satisfied, it is possible for us to experience true intimacy with God as well as healthy relationships with others.

Spiritual safety give us the confidence to honestly be ourselves because we have no fear of abandonment or rejection.

us to fear a loss of control. God's plan is that we find our security in Him. A beautiful word picture of this is found in Psalm 18:2: "The Lord is my rock, my fortress and my deliverer; my God is my rock, in whom I take refuge. He is my shield and the horn [strength] of my salvation, my stronghold." We find another vivid description of security in Psalm 40:2: "He lifted me out of the slimy pit, out of the mud and mire; he set my feet on a rock and gave me a firm place to stand." Both of these passages assure us that no matter what difficulties we face in life, we can trust in our secure foundation in God.

Our confidence in God as our provider also enhances our sense of security. Telling us not to worry about what we will eat or drink and what we will wear, Jesus assures us that our heavenly Father knows what we need. (Matthew 6:25-34)

3. Value - Value, which indicates that we have worth and importance, is essential to the growth of the spirit. One way God shows how much He values us is by giving each of us a calling that no one else can fulfill. He reinforces our value by telling us, "You are the salt of the earth," and "You are the light of the world." (Matthew 5:13-14) But the primary indication of our worth and value in God's eyes is the price He was willing to pay to assure that we would spend eternity with Him: the life of His Son, Jesus Christ.

Circumstances and events can destroy our sense of value. A teenage girl became my client while her parents were going through a divorce as a result of her father's affair with another woman. Melissa, an only child, had previously enjoyed being the center of her parents' lives. Because of the impending divorce, she felt that she was no longer valued by either of her parents.

4. Acceptance - Acceptance is the stamp of unconditional love and approval for who we are, not for what we do, have done, or have not done. We are received and acknowledged for no other reason than for being ourselves. As the direct opposite of judgment, acceptance ignores preferences, preconceived ideas, or any criteria for appraisal. Our Savior demonstrated acceptance when He called the 12 disciples, one by one, even though He knew their weaknesses. He saw Thomas' lack of faith, Peter's inflated ego, and Matthew's love of money, as well as Judas' tendency to betrayal. He called them as they were, not requiring or demanding they first change to please or accommodate Him.

5. Nurturing - Nurturing is the giving of care, comfort, encouragement, affection, guidance, and strength. It can be expressed through physical touch, words of encouragement, and/

20

or acts that express concern. A pat on the back, a hug, a handshake, a card or letter, a hospital visit — all provide nurture and enrich the spirit. But when nurturing is withheld, the spirit withers.

In the Bible, Christ nurtures others on many occasions. One example occurs when He weeps with Mary and Martha after the death of their brother Lazarus. (John 11:33-35) Our Lord also expressed care and compassion when He spoke words of comfort, encouragement, and understanding to those who mourn, who are poor in spirit, and who are persecuted. (Matthew 5:3, 4, 10)

6. **Understanding** - Understanding requires perception and discernment of our human needs. We can be confident that Christ knows and relates to all of our needs because He experienced them firsthand in His incarnation. While living in the flesh on earth, He withstood temptation, hunger, thirst, and betrayal. He grieved for a friend who died. His earthly family thought He should be locked up. People who had watched Him grow up had no confidence in Him. His closest friends did not understand Him. He suffered false accusations, condemnation, and physical pain and suffering. No matter what we are suffering, we know that Christ offers us empathetic understanding.

7. **Forgiveness** - Forgiveness is essential to the health of our spirit, for all of us sin and fall short of the glory of God. (Romans 3:23) Because of God's love, mercy, and grace, we can be forgiven when we fail. No matter what we've done, God's love for us remains intact, but the restoration of our relationship with Him required the redemptive work of the cross.

Jesus teaches about forgiveness in the parable of the Prodigal Son (Luke 15:11-32). Not only does the youngest son betray his father's love by demanding his inheritance before his father's death, he takes the money and spends it in ways contrary to his father's values. Ultimately, he finds himself penniless and groveling with pigs for his food. Realizing his mistakes, he returns, asking his father for forgiveness. Not only does the father welcome him home and reject his offer to work as a slave, he throws a great feast in his son's honor. This is the forgiveness that is ours through Christ!

Forgiveness brings healing to our spirit because it restores our relationship with God. After Jesus' arrest, Peter denied knowing Christ three times even though he previously had vowed he would defend Him even if it meant dying with Christ (Mark 14:27-31). After his denial, Peter wept bitterly. (Mark 14:72) Following Jesus' death and burial, a young man appears to the three women who had come to the tomb to anoint Christ's body with spices.

Understanding requires perception and discernment of our human needs.

Forgiveness brings healing to our spirit because it restores our relationship with God.

Our first bonding is with Christ.

"Quick, tell me about God before you forget."

Infants come into the world with all their spiritual needs met by their Heavenly Father. As they are "handed over" to their earthly parents, it becomes the parents' responsibility to love and nurture their children to the best of their ability.

(Mark 16:5- 7) The young man, whom we understand to be an angel, tells them, "But go, tell his disciples and Peter, 'He is going ahead of you into Galilee . . . .' " For Peter, the message gave the assurance, "Everything is all right between us. I have forgiven you. Our relationship is restored."

8. Belonging - Belonging means being connected in a relationship. It is about intimacy, closeness, and desirability. Without these, a person feels isolated and different. Christ reveals the extent of our belonging when He tells us, "I no longer call you servants, . . . Instead, I have called you friends . . . " (John 15:15) He also says, "For whoever does the will of my Father in heaven is my brother and sister and mother." (Matthew 12:50) What a wonderful description of our "new" family in Christ!

As wonderful as a family relationship is, the greatest degree of belonging is unity. It is Christ's desire for us that we experience oneness with Him and God the Father. (John 17:20-23)

The bonding of Christ's love

Shortly after my daughter, Meredith, was born, my mother rushed into the hospital room, lovingly held her grandchild in her arms, and said, "Quick, tell me about God before you forget." I didn't have to ask Mother what she meant. This tiny infant was bonded to God, just as she was bonded to me, from the moment I conceived her. While in the womb, Meredith's physical needs were supported by my body. At the same time, her spiritual needs were met by her loving Heavenly Father.

God created us for kingdom living, not a life of mediocrity and suffering. In order to experience kingdom living, though, we must follow the requirement of being born again. (John 3:3) Instead of reentering our mother's womb, we need to reenter the spiritual womb through our relationship with Jesus Christ, embrace the fullness of His love, and experience our oneness with Him.

In the hymn "Standing on the Promises," there is a verse referring to our being "bound to Him eternally by love's strong cord." Christ's love is the spiritual "umbilical cord" that supplies all that our spirit needs to sustain good health. If we don't stay connected to it, we flounder in the storms of life.

Belonging means being connected in a relationship.

We need to reenter the spiritual womb through our relationship with Jesus Christ, embrace the fullness of His love, and experience our oneness with Him.

Christ's love is the spiritual "umbilical cord" that supplies all that our spirit needs to sustain good health.

The Effect of Our Expectations

Our experiences in life shape our expectations about the way spiritual needs are met. Look below to see which expectation(s) describes you.

All of these preclude the presence and grace of Christ.

- **I must fix myself.** - This attitude of self-sufficiency is rooted in disappointment and the inability to trust others. Its primary driving emotions are anger and fear. This attituded is prompted by performance-based perfectionism.

- **I must fix others.** - A controlling attitude sometimes develops along with the self-sufficiency noted above. It is prompted by a need to please people, and results in feelings of fear, stress, and being overwhelmed.

- **Others must fix me.** - Rooted in feelings of helpless dependency, this attitude has a wide range of manifestations, from neediness to persistent demanding to manipulation. The driving emotions are fear and shame. This person is "spoiled," getting what they want, but not what they need. Their spirit is never truly satisfied or filled.

- **I can't be fixed.** - Underlying this defeatist thinking is resignation and hopelessness caused by trauma and/or disappointment. Its primary emotions are pain, shame, and fear.

- **My needs are not important.** - This attitude of self-denial grows out of not feeling valued because of experiences of neglect, lack of nurture, or abandonment. It is characterized by numbness and the feeling of being ignored and insignificant.

- **Christ will fix me.** - A healthy confidence in Christ as the fulfiller of all our spiritual needs develops as we embrace His love, grace, and real presence with us.

False and unrealistic expectations about the meeting of our spiritual needs will distract us from our faith in God. But if we allow the Great Physician to cleanse, heal, and fill our wounded spirit, He will enable us to be who God created us to be . . . and enable us to love others as He loves us.

Chapter 3
Spirit Wounds

"My soul is in anguish.
How long, O Lord, how long?" Psalm 6:3

A wound to our spirit is anything that negatively affects our understanding of God's love for us, our relationship with Christ, our recognition of our worth and value in God's eyes, our God-created individuality, and/or our meaning and purpose in life. Some wounds begin subtly as a series of "abrasions," while others may be caused by sudden, violent "attack." Regardless of the means, intensity or duration, the end result of the wound is damage to the God-ordained, foundational truth about who we are as God's child.

Our spirit is wounded in two ways: The first is by wounds to the mind, heart, and body passing through to the spirit. The second way is by starving the spirit of its needs.

The end result of the wound is damage to the God-ordained, foundational truth about who we are as God's child.

Wounds passed through mind, heart, and body

Wounds passed through the mind to the spirit usually result from our inability to find rational solutions to our problems or definitive answers to our questions about life and the events that impact us. When we can't come up with an answer that satisfies us, we get upset. Consider, for example, the pain and turmoil we experience when a child is diagnosed with leukemia or a friend is killed by a drunk driver. We want to know <u>why</u> this happened. When there are no answers, we are driven to hold someone responsible and, in the end, blame ourselves, others, or God. This condemnation results in a wound to our spirit.

Since our heart reflects the state of our relationship between others and ourselves, it should be no surprise that disappointment or anger in a relationship may result in a wound to our heart. This wound, then, passes through to our spirit. A woman who was sexually abused as a child by her father has not only suffered physically, but she has experienced traumatic loss of trust in an essential relationship. As a result, she will have trouble establishing feelings of trust and intimacy with others. It is also very likely that her relationship with her loving Heavenly Father will be negatively affected.

The body, which houses our heart, mind, and spirit, also sustains wounds. This protective, though vulnerable, covering is both visible and accessible to everyone and, as a result, may suffer actual physical damage. These wounds, along with accidental injuries, the ravages of disease, the effects of physical and mental handicaps, and the misuse or abuse of our body, have tremendous impact on our spirit.

Wounds from denial of needs

All of our spiritual needs are met in Christ's unconditional love. But until we acknowledge Him as the source of spiritual fullness and experience intimate fellowship with Him, our needs will be met insufficiently by the way we experience (or don't experience) love from other people. The reality is that no one but our triune God loves perfectly and unconditionally. As a result, we will suffer the hurt of spiritual wounding when we fail to experience safety, security, value, acceptance, nurturing, understanding, forgiveness, and belonging through the love of others. Our instinct is to escape discomfort, but we need to understand that pain in our spirit is an important indication of what needs healing.

I remember an episode of the '60s TV series "Ben Casey" that says a lot about the importance of pain. The story is about a woman who was experiencing intense physical pain in her foot and has surgery to alleviate her suffering. The procedure, in which nerves are cut to prevent transmission of pain impulses to her brain, is a success. As the program closes, we see her stepping on a piece of broken glass as she walks on the beach. Although she is bleeding, the woman continues to walk; for without the sensation of pain, she doesn't know she's been injured. Pain is important because it allows us to identify our wounds so that we can begin to heal them.

One of my clients, Sarah, experienced rejection in her primary relationship from the beginning of her life. Her mother's first full-term pregnancy had resulted in the birth of a baby girl who died shortly after delivery because of a severe congenital defect. When she became pregnant with Sarah shortly after the first baby's death, it was difficult for Sarah's mother to feel any bond with the child she now carried in her womb or to look forward to the baby's birth. Even though Sarah was a healthy, normal baby, her mother did not form a close, loving, nurturing relationship with her.

This experience of rejection communicated with Sarah's spirit and told her she was not valued or accepted. As a result she was unable to value and accept herself, and she came to expect rejection from others. Not only did Sarah fail to receive the nurturing she needed from her mother, but Sarah's sense of belonging was also diminished. During the course of her therapy, the feelings of Sarah's heart provided the clues necessary for her to understand the depth and intensity of the wounds to her spirit.

Imperfect human love

When Christ gave us the new commandment — that we love one another as He loves us (John 13:34) — He made us ambassadors of His love. That is, we are commanded to extend Christ-like, unconditional love to those around us as a way of demonstrating His love to them. When we fail to model Christ's love, not only are we being disobedient, but those who should have received our unconditional love will suffer the consequences as well in the wounding of their spirit.

Parenting is perhaps the most critical role as ambassador of Christ's love, for the parent's expression of love will be their child's initial experience of love. Insofar as a parent fails to love unconditionally, the child's spiritual needs will not be fed, and they will experience spiritual wounds. We are born with "open" and "soft" spirits into an imperfect world where there are no perfect parents. Each generation is shaped by the one preceding it. Regardless of Christ's command to love unconditionally, parents can never completely provide for their child's spirit.

No one can fully meet a person's spiritual needs but Christ — not even parents who are doing their very best under the empowerment of the Holy Spirit. We can help our children the most by loving them to the fullest extent we can and pointing them to God's truth about who they are in Him so that they can find healing and the fulfillment of their spiritual needs.

There are numerous illustrations in this book drawn from the experiences of my clients. While they frequently refer to spiritual woundedness growing out of unhealthy or abusive relationships with parents, I am not engaging in "parent bashing." The parents of these clients are not bad people; they loved to the extent they could based on their own experience of love.

Original wounding

Original wounding of the spirit comes from three sources: Mom, Dad, and life circumstances. All of us have at least one wound from one of these three sources, and most of us have wounds from each source. The more dysfunctional the family or situation in which we grew up, the more wounds we bear. Rules, such as "Don't talk, don't feel, don't trust, and don't be yourself," often operate in dysfunctional families and result in wounds to the spirit.

Each of us must identify our unmet needs because they indicate the original wounds of the spirit. In the following section are six clues that point to our wounds of the spirit. Keep in mind that not all six elements have to be present. We are looking for themes repeated throughout life — the same feelings expressed over and over again.

We are born with "open" and "soft" spirits into an imperfect world where there are no perfect parents.

Parents can never completely provide for their child's spirit.

What causes wounds to our spirit?

1. Wounds to the mind, heart, and body may be passed through to our spirit.

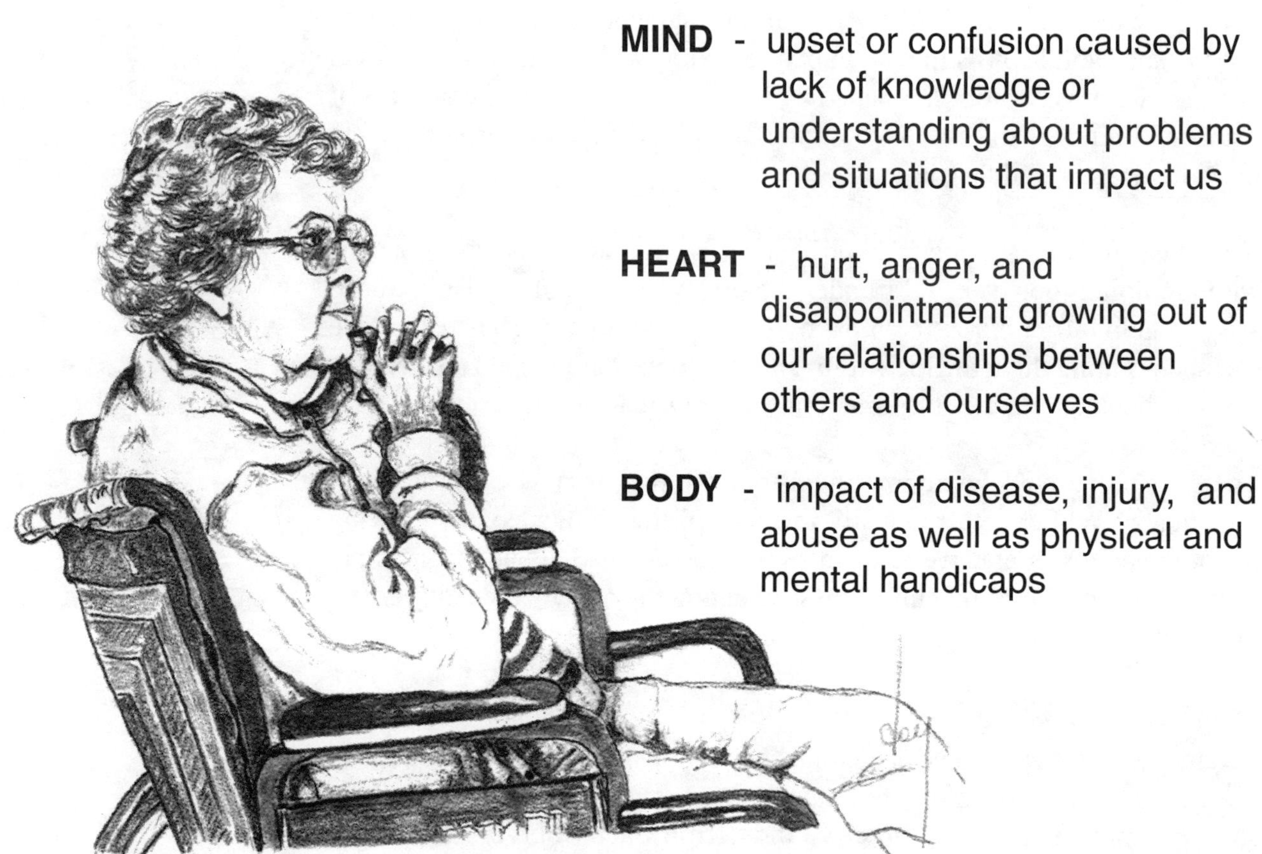

MIND - upset or confusion caused by lack of knowledge or understanding about problems and situations that impact us

HEART - hurt, anger, and disappointment growing out of our relationships between others and ourselves

BODY - impact of disease, injury, and abuse as well as physical and mental handicaps

Some of the wounds to our spirit began as wounds to our mind, heart, or body. For example, our distress over a friend's hurtful comments begins in our heart, but is passed through to our spirit. Likewise, the physical pain we experience from a crippling disease passes through to affect our spirit as well.

Mental, emotional, and physical pain are carried to our spirit by an avenue, which (for lack of a better term) I call a " river." This river is most often one of shame, fear, or blame. The river of shame/fear/blame "interprets" the pain to our spirit. What began as an insensitive comment now means that "Nobody really loves me." And our physical discomfort is distorted by fear into "Now I'm just a burden to my family." As a result, our spirit is wounded as well.

2. Our spirit's needs may have been denied.

SAFETY - from danger, harm, rejection,
                    or abandonment

SECURITY - order, stability, consistency

VALUE - appreciated for worth, merit,
                    importance, desirability

ACCEPTANCE - unconditional approval
                    for who we are

NURTURING - given comfort,
                    encouragement, caring,
                    guidance

UNDERSTANDING - compassionate and
                    sympathetic reception

FORGIVENESS - pardoned from
                    punishment; given grace
                    and redemption

BELONGING - connection; secure
                    relationship

Indicators of unmet needs

There are several indicators that we have unmet needs. These include our resentments; hurts; guilt and/or self-pity; fears; efforts to give what we are lacking; and denial of needs.

1. **Resentments** - Someone who constantly says, "I resent the fact that nobody ever listens to me," may need understanding. Rebellious behavior also provides clues about our resentments and anger.
2. **Hurts** - Feelings of hurt reveal unmet needs. The feeling that "nobody really cares about me" reveals a need for value. Feeling isolated indicates a need for belonging. Our attitudes that arise from feelings, such as " hypersensitivity" or "wearing our feelings on our sleeve," indicate spiritual wounds.
3. **Guilt and/or self-pity** - Feelings of guilt and/or self-pity should be analyzed as clues to spiritual wounds. Thoughts of "There must be something wrong with me" or "I don't deserve . . . " signal spiritual emptiness.
4. **Fears** - Many of us are afraid that we will never be loved, needed, forgiven, accepted, safe, or secure. These fears leave us with a sense of despair. Identifying our fears helps us identify the underlying area of spiritual woundedness.
5. **Efforts to give what we do not have** - An example of this is lavishing nurturing and acceptance on others because we hunger for those qualities ourselves. We are hoping that someone will notice our unspoken desire: "Give me what I'm trying to give you." We need to remember, however, we cannot give what we do not have. Otherwise, we are giving artificially.
6. **Denial of needs** - Expressions, such as "I don't need anybody" and "I don't care whether anyone likes me or not," typify a spirit in need of healing. We have given up on our needs being met for so long that we deny their existence. If we deny we need it, chances are that's exactly what we do need.

These six indicators, separately or in combination, point us to our need of a greater healing.

These six indicators, separately or in combination, point us to our need of a greater healing.

Assignment
Spirit Wounds

1. Identify your unmet needs. Define and describe each unmet need in the space below, making sure you include how each deprivation occurred. If any have become a recurring theme in your life, identify them as such.

2. Identify ways you have tried to meet these unmet needs on your own (e.g., through others, through performance, etc.).

3. Prayerfully imagine yourself crawling up into God's lap. Picture Him holding you as you tell Him about your unmet needs. Let Him comfort you in His loving arms as He tells you how much He cherishes you.

The Stray

You are there
Ready to give, to meet my needs.
My thirst to fill, my hunger to feed.
You are there
Calling me out of the rain,
Waiting to heal my innermost pain.
You are there
Standing with door open wide
Inviting me to come inside.

I am here
In the midst of the rain,
In the midst of the pain.
I am here
Dying, cold, wet and alone.
Longing for a warm, dry home.
I am here
So afraid to leave what I know,
But, oh, how I *want* to go!

I inch down my wall and creep toward You.
Knowing I need You, but fearful, too.
The rain is driving; I can hardly see.
Then I sense arms reaching down for me.
You came to meet me, knowing my fear.
You pick me up and hold me near.
In the midst of the rain I feel so dry.
Understanding, I begin to cry.
You are my shelter; there's love in Your arms.
In Your presence there will be no harm.
Though now I see only in part,
I'm beginning to trust as You show me Your heart.

© Melody 1995

Chapter 4
Self-Protection

"Those controlled by the sinful nature cannot please God."
Romans 8:8

Richard came to me for counseling after his wife left him. Although he was shocked by her departure, he had begun to recognize his role in the failure of their marriage. In time, Richard revealed that his father had been physically abusive and very strict with him. He said that from a very early age he knew that he had to be in control of his life or suffer the consequences. As a result, Richard developed a pattern of taking care of his needs. He became very self-centered and insensitive to the needs of others and was unable to be vulnerable, even with the women he had married.

When our spirits are wounded, we respond by turning to various means of self-preservation. It doesn't matter that we don't understand our discomfort is caused by wounds to our spirit. Our goal is simply to stop the pain or find a way to minimize it. In our wounded state, we look for ways to restore balance and safety. Unfortunately, our woundedness prompts us to make a number of wrong assumptions, and when we act on these wrong beliefs, our misery is only made worse.

Nobody cares; I'll take care of me.
As soon as Jim and Annette sat down in my office, I could feel the tension between them. Jim was withdrawn and absorbed in his work. His workaholic father had never had much time for him despite the fact that Jim had always tried to win his father's approval. Even as an adult, Jim thought the only way his needs could be met was by becoming successful in his father's eyes. Although he continued working for his father, Jim sensed that he still didn't quite measure up.

Annette was a middle child who had not received much attention from either of her parents. In response to this lack of nurture, she learned to protect herself by being angry, aggressive, and demanding. When Jim didn't meet her needs, Annette directed her rage at him. Essentially, both were encased in thick shells that prevented any degree of vulnerability and intimacy.

When our spirits are wounded, we respond by turning to various means of self-preservation.

Our goal is simply to stop the pain or find a way to minimize it.

Whether consciously or unconsciously, we first assume that, since our needs were not met or we were hurt, God must be mad at us. Our feelings are: "God doesn't care about me; He won't meet my needs; God is punishing me; or He has withdrawn from me." We also project these same ideas onto other people, saying, "She must be mad at me," or "If he really cared about me, . . ."

After we've convinced ourselves that neither God nor anyone else cares about us, we take on a responsibility God never intended us to have: We begin taking charge of our lives, and excluding others, especially God. We become responsible for meeting all our spiritual needs or use manipulation to give that responsibility to others.

At this point, our spirit is defended, not protected. It may not be open to attack, but neither is it open to healing. For once we take over meeting these needs, our spirit becomes so encrusted we lose sight of God's design for us — that the needs of our spirit are to be met <u>only</u> by Him.

Protected by will power

In order to protect ourselves, we may take measures, albeit ineffectively, to defend our heart, body, and mind through will power. We may expend a lot of time, effort, and money to look good on the outside so that no one knows we are hurting on the inside. Emotionally distancing ourselves from others also insulates our hearts.

Physically distancing ourselves from others can be a means of protecting our body. Another, less obvious approach to defending our body is through loss or gain of weight, "makeovers," and clothing choices. We try to protect our mind by being task- or behavior-oriented, trying to "do it right" as a means of solving life's problems. We try to make people happy, "play politics" with others, or set standards of perfection for ourselves that cannot possibly be attained and only lead to further feelings of inadequacy.

Through the process of protecting heart, body, and mind, we become increasingly self-centered as we go out of our way to avoid discomfort. And when we finally realize that we live in a world where both pain and disappointment are virtual certainties, we may withdraw into ourselves and quit taking risks.

Operating styles

Self-protection is exhibited in a number of ways, and most of us display a combination of them. The first operating style is that of <u>maintaining a defensive stance</u>, as described above. Unfortunately, when we expend our energy defending ourselves, we are unable to listen to, or empathize with, others. A second manifestation is that of <u>actively attacking others</u>. We might also <u>withdraw from others</u> by keeping aloof and distant from them, both physically and emotionally. We make decisions such as: "I'll never trust anyone again. I'll never let anyone get close to me."

Ouch! Anyplace but HERE, Lord.

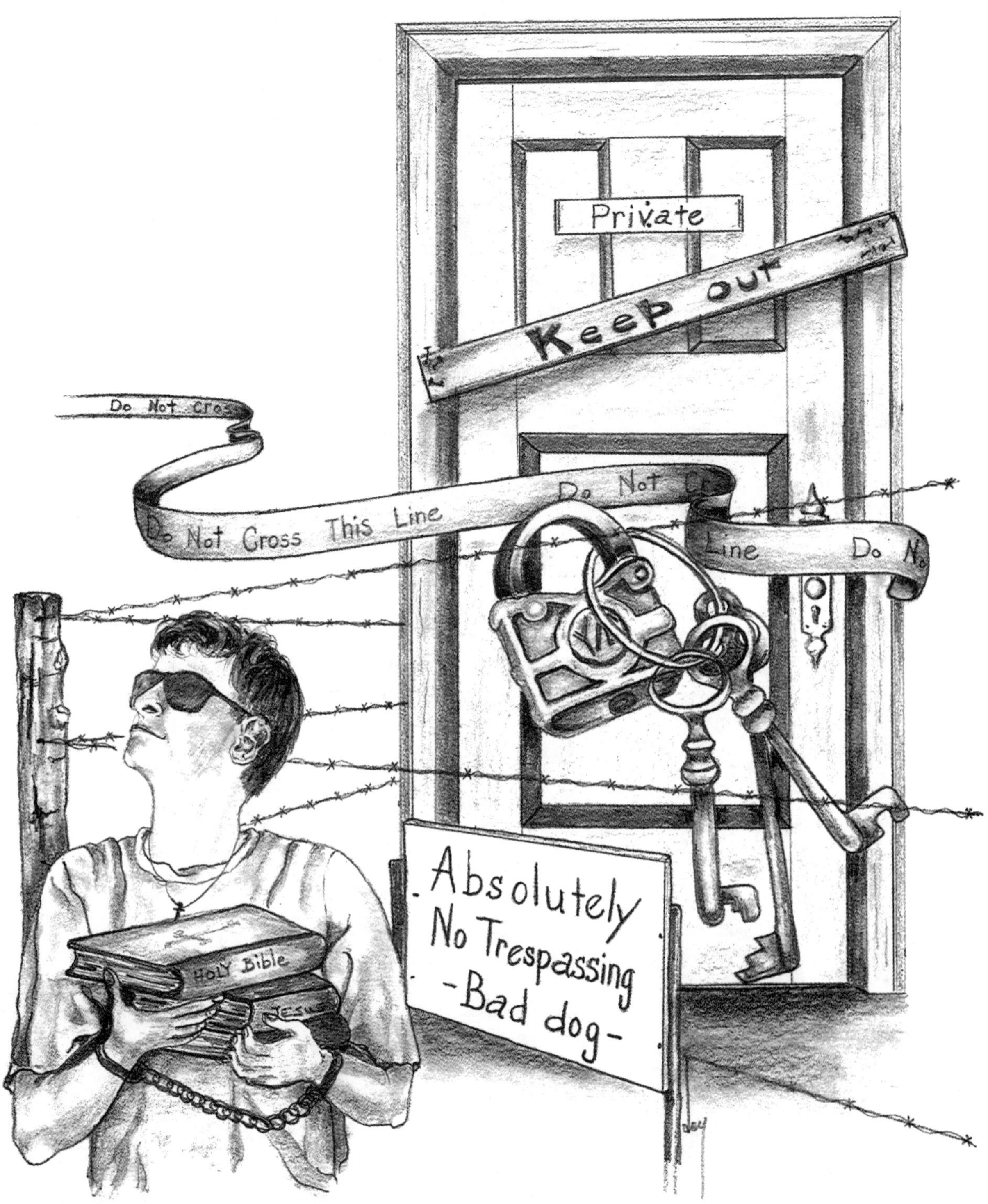

We gladly let Christ into most areas of our lives. It's those private places that we desperately try to shield from Him that keep us from being completely filled by the Holy Spirit. What's keeping you shackled?

Another style of self-protection involves "<u>wearing a mask</u>." Hiding the real self from exposure, we go through the motions of being what we think others expect of us. Finally, some individuals exhibit a <u>hardened heart</u> that does not allow anyone to be close or connected in any way. Having taken withdrawal to its extreme, we cannot relate, understand, or empathize with others, and relationships become impossible because we have become emotionally insensitive. As a result, communication becomes destructive.

Lies and secrets

Because we rely on them to negate truth or manipulate the reality of what causes our pain, lies and secrets are major implements in the arsenal of self-protection. Dishonesty can function as a weapon of either defense or offense, and may also be used in a more specialized form of denial, as we attempt to lie to ourselves with regard to actual circumstances or events. We keep secrets as a way of controlling opinions and consequences. By keeping silent about the darker side of our lives, such as addictions, sexual abuse, or spousal battery, we try to prevent others and ourselves from feeling shame.

We do it to ourselves.

The tragic result of our efforts to protect ourselves is that, instead of achieving safety and security, we feel more and more like victims. For while we are fearfully guarding ourselves against rejection, abandonment, failure, powerlessness, and being controlled, we are continuing to ignore or deny the needs of our spirit. Thus, self-protection results in further wounding, and we feel increasingly worthless, helpless, and hopeless. The enemy is now within us, and our spirit is dying.

Lies and secrets are major implements in the arsenal of self-protection.

The tragic result of our efforts to protect ourselves is that we feel more and more like victims.

Self-protection results in further wounding, and we feel increasingly worthless, helpless, and hopeless.

Assignment
Self-Protection

1. Describe the negative feelings you have about God. These may include anger, fear, and hurt.

2. Describe, honestly, the characteristics you think God possesses and how He acts and relates to us — and to you in particular.

Chapter 5
Self-inflicted Spiritual Damage

"Those who live according to the sinful nature have their minds set on what that nature desires . . ." Romans 8:5

If someone says we have a bad attitude or need an "attitude adjustment," they are commenting on the state of our spirit. For when we try to protect ourselves from, or compensate for, our spiritual woundedness, we develop spiritually damaging dispositions and traits that mar the health of our spirit. Each characterizes an approach to life — a stance as opposed to a feeling — that revolves around self instead of around God, as He designed us to be centered. These harmful attitudes become pervasive — permeating our outlook on life, shaping our response to people and events, and blinding us to God's truth about us. They also keep us from seeing our underlying wounds.

Our attitude reflects the state of our spirit.

In our woundedness, we allow ourselves to be "identified" by the feelings related to our damaging dispositions. If, for example, shame becomes the characteristic that describes us, it becomes our "truth." Unfortunately, when we act and react out of our woundedness in ways that do not reflect the image of God and God's truth, we are sinning. Regardless of the fact that we feel very justified in having these attitudes, they are sinful nevertheless. For this reason we must repent and be cleansed of our spiritually damaging dispositions and traits in order to be healed.

Victim of our attitude
Keith wanted to leave his wife of 30 years when he came to me for marriage counseling. In time I came to recognize that this 50-year-old man was paralyzed by fear and full of anger, resentment, and bitterness. A people-pleaser who was afraid to be himself, Keith could not be honest and responsible. He could not initiate conversation or relationship, nor could he communicate honestly about his feelings. The grip of fear was so strong that even when confronted with the truth about himself over the course of several years of counseling, Keith was unwilling and unable to reach out to his wife and share with her. Although his original goal was to save the marriage, his fear would not let him do what was required. In the end, his marriage failed.

Spiritually damaging dispositions and traits are the strongholds through which we are tempted to deny our rightful identity as God's precious child. When we experience conversion and are cleansed of our sins, we enter a restored relationship with Christ. Conversion, however, does not bring us to perfection. We still have to deal with these destructive attitudes. Although our own struggle may not be as crippling as Keith's battle with fear, resentment, and bitterness, we must recognize that we _all_ have damaging traits. Acknowledging their presence is the first step in winning the battle.

I have identified eight spiritually damaging dispositions and traits: shame, fear, bitterness/resentment, denial/dishonesty, pride/control, judgmentalism/critical spirit, self-centeredness, and unforgiveness.

1. Shame

Shame is a spiritually damaging attitude that arises from a loss of relationship, innocence, hopes, dreams, or health. The triggering event may be death, divorce, abuse, illness, accident, or some other life-changing circumstance that threatens our security with God, self, or others. When we have been wounded in this way, shame is how we "make sense" of our hurt and loss; it becomes for us an "interpreter" of all that happens in our life. It causes us to believe that we are responsible for the event, and that we are, therefore, bad, unlovable, insignificant, and/or unworthy.

Unchallenged, these lies we believe about ourselves overtake us and prevent us from grasping God's truth about who we really are. Instead of knowing we are God's precious child, we feel that we have no value to Him or anyone else. It is as though we are traveling a river of shame through life.

Physical, emotional, mental, and spiritual manifestations of shame provide clues that help us identify that we experience shame. Physical manifestations of shame include muscle tension; heart rate increase; head-, neck- and backache; exhaustion; nausea; indigestion; heartburn; and general stomach tension. Shame manifests itself in the emotions as anxiety, panic, confusion, embarrassment, emotional numbness, and anger.

Mental messages, such as "Why can't I do anything right? What's wrong with me? Nothing ever changes. I don't matter, and nobody cares," may indicate shame. Spiritual messages of shame focus on our relationship with Christ. These include such beliefs as: "God is mad at me. He's punishing me. He's disappointed in me. God can't forgive me for this. He has abandoned me."

In general, shame isolates, judges, confuses, and robs us of joy, peace, hope, and love. Shame will not let us win! The stories of Peter and Judas best summarize the effects of shame. Peter denied Christ; Judas betrayed Christ. Peter repented and was transformed into a true disciple. Judas, instead, hanged himself. He said, in effect, "I am beyond redemption. I cannot be forgiven or healed."

It is critical that we recognize our shame. If left uncovered, shame can make us give up on the redemptive power of Christ and, in the process, give up on ourselves. We have a choice: to be partners with Christ in the healing process — to let Him dam up the river of shame — or to allow that river to continue carrying wounds to our spirit.

2. Fear

 We experience fear in two forms. The first is a "feeling" of fear, and the second is an "attitude" of fear. Feeling fear is related to a specific incident, such as a large snake crawling near us. The resulting feeling of fear, in this case, might be followed by the instinctive reaction of either fight or flight.

The attitude of fear, on the other hand, may characterize our approach to life. Looking at life through the eyes of fear, we recoil from risk-taking. We are afraid of abandonment, rejection, failure, being controlled, and being out of control. We may even be afraid of success. Paralyzed by our attitude of fear, we shirk our responsibility of becoming the person God meant us to be. That is why fear as an attitude damages our spirit.

Paralyzed by our attitude of fear, we shirk our responsibility of becoming the person God meant us to be.

Although Betty made appointments for counseling every week, she frequently called to reschedule, especially after I gave her an assignment or confronted her with the need to grow in her spiritual life. As a result of her feelings of incompetence and inadequacy, Betty was stuck and made no meaningful progress. She could even talk about her "stuckness," which was just another name for fear. Afraid to risk success in being more alive, she remained bound by fear, unable to do what God called her to do.

3. Bitterness/Resentment

When we harbor anger and unforgiveness because our spirit has been wounded or its needs are not being met, we become bitter and resentful. These spiritually damaging dispositions crust over our spirit and harden our heart. As a result, we approach life from an attitude of blame. We expect to be hurt, and so we remain defensive.

When we harbor anger and unforgiveness, we become bitter and resentful.

The barrier of bitterness and resentment creates a self-fulfilling prophecy. We expect to be wounded, and others are afraid of our anger. When they withdraw, our belief that we will be rejected has been verified. Bitter, resentful people are like porcupines. Their attitude makes them untouchable, and they become used to attacking others. They are certainly not living the life Christ wants for them: a life expressing love.

4. Denial/Dishonesty

The spiritually damaging trait of denial/dishonesty refers to hiding, or being dishonest about, one's true self. When we deny who we really are, we give up our sense of self and become like the chameleon who takes on the colors of its environment. We rarely acknowledge or express feelings of our own and take our cues from what other people want us to think and to be like. As a result, we hide both our needs and our abilities.

Spiritually Damaging Dispositions and Traits

We develop a hard turtle shell of spiritually damaging dispositions and traits to hold us together so that we can deal with life. The shell hides our secrets, covers our deficiencies, and gives the illusion of strength and safety. Too often, it is only when life "flips us over" and we lie helpless on our backs that we finally call for help.

Just as the tough shell on this little turtle is a barrier around his body, our self-protective shell forms a constricting barrier around our spirit. Unlike the turtle's shell, though, which is part of God's design, our spiritually damaging traits and dispositions prevent us from participating in God's plan. He wants us to trust Him for the protection of our spirit. Is it any wonder, then, that we can't feel God's love for us when we rely on ourselves for protection rather than on God?

When we have an underlying attitude of fear of rejection and/or abandonment, we may find it impossible to take the risk of revealing who we are, even to the people closest to us. Fearing the vulnerability of honesty, we become "people pleasers" in order to get others to like us.

The middle child of stern, emotionless parents, John learned the best way to survive was to engage in "mind reading" to identify and meet the needs of others. Because family members often ridiculed him, he kept his own thoughts, feelings, needs, and opinions to himself. He and his wife, Rachel, came to my office for counseling to help them communicate better.

Angry and hurt, Rachel complained that John shut her out of his life. John, on the other hand, felt frustrated because he couldn't please her. She wanted to know him; he only wanted to avoid confrontation. John's spiritually damaging trait of dishonesty was a way of hiding his own emptiness. Afraid of Rachel's rejection, he never committed himself to any decision or responsibility in the marriage, which left Rachel feeling abandoned and alone. John's destructive disposition kept him from displaying the fullness of who he was created to be. He was, in effect, "hiding his lamp under a bowl." (Matthew 5:14-15)

5. Pride/Control

Underlying this spiritually damaging disposition is oftentimes a wound of outright rejection or, at the least, conditional love and acceptance. As a consequence, we determine that if we are good enough, we will receive the love we need, the approval we want, the security we've been denied, etc. On the other hand, we may decide that we'll be "bad" enough so that others won't love us. The ultimate control issue is about love: We try to control others to make them love us or not love us. For some it relates to God's love. Since it is His nature to love, we can't make God love us more by being good or make Him love us less by rebelling against Him.

When we are controlling, we are trying to establish a sense of safety, stability, predictability, and structure as if an I-centered life can create them through our own relentless determination to have our needs met our way. Control performs and manipulates, while pride believes "I can meet my needs on my own!"

Perfectionism is a manifestation of pride/control, but it brings only conditional satisfaction because it is based on the principle that says, "I will get my needs met _if_ I'm good enough." Whenever we experience an upset to the order we have created, we struggle to regain balance by controlling and manipulating both outside circumstances and other people.

Control and shame are most often two sides of one coin. Shame says, "I'm a failure," while control says, "But next time, . . . " The list of options finishing this resolution might include " I will act better" or "I will be better." Control believes in a magic formula guaranteeing a perfect life. The problem lies in figuring out the formula, when in reality, there is none. We are not, and never have been, in control.

Pride/control is characterized by a pattern of self- sufficient behavior. Susan grew up in a home with an alcoholic father and a mother who spent all her energy taking care of him. Susan learned how to be self-sufficient and distrustful of her parents. Her parents were not dependable, so Susan came to believe that she could not depend on anyone but herself. Pride — arrogance — became an easy defense. As she grew older, Susan convinced herself that she could do anything, and that she did not need anyone, not even God.

Another manifestation of pride is the attitude of rebellion or defiance. The person exhibiting this characteristic realizes God has authority, but refuses to submit to Him or to others in authority. Too often, a rebellious person will become self- destructive, which can cause other people to withdraw, leaving the rebel feeling isolated. But because of pride, the individual blames the self-destruction on others. A vicious cycle of rebellion, self-destruction, isolation, and blame is thus set in motion.

Although we may feel or believe otherwise, we simply <u>cannot control</u> God's love for us, our worth and value, or other people's love for us. Breaking the shame/control cycle begins with accepting that truth.

6. *Judgmentalism/Critical Spirit*

The sixth spiritually damaging disposition is judgmentalism and a critical spirit. It is at the root of our racial, ethnic, and other prejudices, as well as the driving force behind our assessment of a person's character on the basis of their dress, possessions, success, failure, and actions. While the Bible tells us not to judge others, I believe it is saying that although we can form an opinion about a person's behavior, we are not to judge their heart. In other words, we can assess as wrong what a person has done, but we have no right to make assumptions about that individual's value, purpose, meaning, or intent.

We can assess as wrong what a person has done, but we have no right to make assumptions about that individual's value, purpose, meaning, or intent.

When we assume there's a hidden meaning behind complimentary words that are said about us instead of accepting the praise as sincere, for example, we are judging the individual's heart. It is also possible to be guilty of judging our own heart, such as declaring ourselves to be worthless on the basis of the guilt we feel because of our behavior. Christ alone has the right to judge both ourselves and others.

Judgmentalism drives a critical spirit; that is, because we are judgmental, we may become predisposed to being critical of life, self, and others. In the extreme, we begin churning inside with our criticism before others open their mouths or perhaps even before they show up!

There is, oftentimes, an intergenerational aspect to having a judgmental, critical spirit, such as having grown up with someone who was a critical perfectionist. This destructive trait also manifests as a way for individuals who think very negatively about themselves to feel better by characterizing someone else as far worse. For others, this destructive attitude serves as a form of self-punishing penance.

7. Self-centeredness

Self-centeredness is another spiritually damaging trait, and it often accompanies pride. When we try to take care of our spiritual wounds alone, we become single-minded. Fearful that no one else cares enough to help us, we focus all our energy on our woundedness and meeting our own needs. Our prideful self-sufficiency keeps us from believing that anyone <u>can</u> help us.

Our prideful self-sufficiency keeps us from believing that anyone <u>can</u> help us.

There is also a connection between self-centeredness, shame, control, and fear. For example, if our response to a wound to our spirit is an attitude of fear and shame, we may be self-centered and controlling as a way of establishing value and security. Self-centeredness also creates barriers in our relationships with others because it blinds us to their hurts. Our pain is more important than anything or anyone else.

8. Unforgiveness

Unforgiveness reflects a spirit hardened by bitterness, resentment, and judgmentalism — a spirit that holds onto grudges and the hurts experienced in life. In fact, unforgiveness may be an expression of judgmentalism "to the max," a condemnation that withholds forgiveness because we have determined the other person doesn't deserve it. Rather than turning the other cheek or giving another chance, we say, in effect, "One strike and you're out of my life!"

Unforgiveness reflects a spirit hardened by bitterness, resentment, and judgmentalism.

Sometimes our hostility and blame are directed toward the persons or entities we see as the "offending party," but we may also exhibit unforgiveness as a foundational disposition because we cannot forgive life in general for our disappointments. Our unforgiving attitude may drive us to seek revenge for wrongs of the past or, at least, exact some sort of "payment." Needless to say, when we are bound by an unforgiving attitude, the principle of grace is inconceivable.

Labels

The seemingly casual comments others make about us can reveal a lot about our underlying spiritually damaging attitudes. The following are just a few of the more obvious reflections of an unhealthy spirit:

chip on his shoulder ➡	resentment/bitterness
afraid of her shadow ➡	fear
wears her feelings on her sleeve ➡	shame
looking out for No.1 ➡	self-centeredness
picky, picky, picky! ➡	judgmental, critical spirit

Addictions

1. Alcohol

2. Drugs

3. Food

4. Responsibility

5. Work

6. Perfectionism

Addictions are any habits, preoccupations, practices, or activities that keep us out of communion with God, self, and others. We use them to try to satisfy unmet needs and cover our pain and guilt. Because they blind us to our spiritually damaging dispositions and traits, addictions further choke our spirit.

Addictions

In addition to our spiritually damaging dispositions and traits, we also develop addictions. These habits, preoccupations, practices, or activities keep us out of communion with God, self, and others. Because an addiction takes God's place in our life, it overrides God's ordained plan and purpose for us. While we more readily recognize addictions to alcohol, drugs, food, work, responsibility, or perfectionism, the truth is that we are all addicted to something in some form.

We use addictions as a way of satisfying our unmet needs, covering the pain that results from our unmet needs, and helping us avoid the threat that our needs will not be met. When we are not able to control our world and be completely safe, both emotionally and rationally, we try to escape or avoid our pain through addictions. We also avoid the pain of our guilt through the use of addictions.

Regardless of the type of addiction or the nature of our unmet need, the focus is the same: coping, surviving — just trying to "get by." Unfortunately, our addictions may also blind us to our destructive dispositions and traits, acting as detours to keep us "off-track" and away from a transforming relationship with Christ. Addictions will never give us the abundant life that Christ describes. Only Christ can remove our spiritually damaging traits; only Christ can bring us abundant life.

Having spiritually damaging dispositions and traits does NOT mean that we are defective, but these self-protective coverings do inhibit us from being the person God intends us to be. Unfortunately, some people are so enveloped that they confuse who they really are with their destructive attitude. This is because spiritually damaging dispositions and traits act as a binding around our spirits. Although they may offer some protection from further pain, they do not heal us, for in the end they choke our spirits. We are bound as tightly as Lazarus was in his grave cloths. Just as Christ came and set him free from death, it is Christ alone who can free us from the bondage of our spiritually damaging dispositions and traits.

Assignment
Self-inflicted Spiritual Damage

1. Identify your spiritually damaging dispositions and traits. Describe these attitudes and tell how you continue to justify them.

2. Write a "Declaration of Independence" from these destructive attitudes.

3. Identify your addictions. Describe the purposes they serve and how they act as substitutes for God.

4. Identify and describe how your spiritually damaging dispositions and traits have damaged yourself, others, and your relationship with God.

5. Write <u>one</u> of the following:
   (a) a letter accepting God's gift of grace
   (b) a letter saying that Christ's blood is not enough to cleanse you

Chapter 6
Awareness

"For I know my transgressions,
and my sin is always before me."　Psalm 51:3

Do you remember the parable of the wedding feast described in Matthew 22:1-14? It is the story of the king who invited guests to an elaborate banquet to celebrate his son's wedding. The first people who were invited refused to come because they were too busy taking care of their own affairs. Although nothing they were doing could have compared with what the king offered them, they chose to deny the king's power and ignore his generosity.

We are like these guests when we don't respond to God's invitation to come to Him for the satisfaction of our spiritual needs — continuing instead to seek fulfillment through performance, achievement, and success. And in our stubborn arrogance and ignorance, we reject the Bread of Life.

 A second group of people responded to the king's invitation, but among them was a man who remained dressed in attire that was inappropriate for such a wonderful occasion. Although it was customary in this period of Biblical history for wedding guests to wear special garments provided by their host, he rejected the king's clothing and, as a result, was sent away.

We are like this man when we clothe our spirits inappropriately with shame, fear, bitterness and resentment, denial and dishonesty, pride and control, judgmentalism and a critical spirit, self-centeredness, and unforgiveness. In so doing, we reject God's gift of His esteem for us and our value in His eyes. If we come before Christ shrouded in our self-destructive attitudes, we will not be able to stay for the feast of joy that comes with Christ's invitation to healing. We <u>must</u> surrender our self-protection in order to receive true spirit-protection.

We <u>must</u> surrender our self-protection in order to receive true spirit-protection.

First, we must acknowledge the fact that we have spiritual needs and that some of these needs have not been met. Next, we must recognize the wounded state of our spirits caused by our unmet spiritual needs and the traumas that result from living in a fallen world. Then, we need to accept our dependence on Christ for healing these wounds.

Laura was career-minded. She and her husband of 20 years had no children, and through the years they had settled into a dull routine of work, separate physical fitness routines, and a January ski trip. Laura put in long hours at the office and spent several days each month traveling to her company's branch locations. On one of these business trips, she felt a strong attraction to a fellow manager whom she had met at a corporate meeting. He seemed to understand the pressures of the business and offered her a sympathetic ear. Their encounter was limited to conversation over drinks, but Laura recognized the underlying tension between them and the fact that she was at risk for having an affair.

In counseling, Laura began to acknowledge her deep, aching need for value, security, and belonging. She saw that when her husband had not met those needs, she had turned to career for self-satisfaction, which still left her feeling empty. Laura's awareness that her spiritual needs had not been met by her husband or her career enabled her to step out in faith to let Christ meet all her spiritual needs.

Dependent upon Christ

Let's look at the story of Nicodemus. (John 3:1-17) Like all Pharisees, this learned man relied on his adherence to the Jewish law for his salvation. He must have had doubts about the reliability of this approach, for Nicodemus went to Jesus secretly one night to learn what he needed to do to get to heaven. In reality he wanted to know how he could reach heaven through his own efforts.

Jesus' answer was shocking: "I tell you the truth, no one can see the kingdom of God unless he is born again." (John 3:3) Since Nicodemus only knew about taking care of and protecting himself through his own efforts, this requirement for rebirth through the Spirit made no sense. He had no understanding of his unmet needs of the spirit or of his dependence upon Christ. Like this Pharisee, we look all around us for something to fill our unmet needs and revive our wounded spirit, never expecting to have to be dependent upon Christ.

Barriers around heart, body, and mind

Since we are made up of four parts (heart, body, mind, and spirit), our desire to prevent hurts and disappointments prompts us to put barriers around each part of ourselves. To prevent emotional pain and hurtful feelings, we put walls around our hearts. We refuse to get close to others in a relationship, saying, "I'm not going to trust anybody," or "I'm not going to let anybody get close enough to hurt me." To protect ourselves physically, we may put the barrier of distance around our bodies, refusing to let anyone get close enough for physical contact, or we may dress or behave in ways that keep people at a distance. Trying to protect our minds results in insulating ourselves from both lies and truth. As we refuse to hear any new ideas or information, we say, in effect, "Don't confuse me with the facts; my mind is already made up!"

We look all around us for something to fill our unmet needs and revive our wounded spirit, never expecting to have to be dependent upon Christ.

Growing into Christ's Likeness

One of the greatest joys in life is loving and being loved. We grow in our ability to love when we become vulnerable to Christ and allow Him to pour His love into us. Why not lay aside your mask of self-protection? It doesn't work anyway. Ask Christ to literally *soak* you in His love and experience what real protection is all about!

Although many of us fail to acknowledge our spiritual component, we may subconsciously protect our spiritual selves by erecting a barrier that allows us to avoid teachings that would lead us to confront our sinful nature. By using this "filter," we can separate "feel good" teachings from those that convict.

Each of these self-protective barriers gives the illusion of preventing further discomfort. Instead, the barriers actually keep out healing as well as cause further infection of our wounds. For at the same time we seek protection behind our walls, shame and other spiritually damaging dispositions — which operate within the barriers — are attacking our spirit. As a result, we continue to believe the lies about ourselves, others, and Christ while we try to find healing on our own terms.

Sometimes we seek healing through others; however, our well is far too empty for others to be able to fill or satisfy us. Even when people try to give us what we say we need from them, shame robs us of the healing power by preventing us from accepting their efforts to help us. For example, you may tell your husband that you wish he would send you roses, and he does. Then you think, "It doesn't count; I had to tell him." Or, you say to a friend, "I wish my husband would call me every day from work and check on me." When he does call four out of five days, your response is, "See, he doesn't care. He didn't call every day."

If we place walls around our heart, body, mind, and spirit, yet still rely on others to fill our emptiness, they truly cannot help us. We can only find wholeness by recognizing our woundedness and seeking healing in Christ first, for **He alone can perfectly satisfy us**. Then we must adopt Christ's attitude toward us: both accepting the truth that Christ values us in order to value ourselves, and believing that He forgives us so that we can forgive ourselves. Only then can we allow others to help meet our needs. Their efforts will be like icing on the cake of what has already been accomplished through Christ. For when we allow Christ to fill our empty well, the affirmation of others adds to that fullness.

Holy Spirit protection empowers

Despite the fact that our spirit is constantly assaulted by the events of life, the Holy Spirit is the only shield of defense we need. His enveloping presence protects as well as nourishes our spirit. As our spiritual health is restored, we can increasingly accept our new identity in Christ and take hold of our God-intended value, meaning, and purpose.

It is on this foundation of spiritual integrity that we are empowered to build healthy physical, mental, and emotional boundaries that help protect us from abusive relationships. Unlike the hard shell of damaging traits described in Chapter 5, which only inhibit our healing, boundaries define what is acceptable and unacceptable in our interaction with others, based on our wholeness in Christ. They provide some protection from inappropriate

Each of these self-protective barriers gives the illusion of preventing further discomfort. Instead, the barriers actually keep out healing as well as cause further infection of our wounds.

The Holy Spirit is the only shield of defense we need. His enveloping presence protects as well as nourishes our spirit.

physical contact and the manipulative emotions and damaging behaviors of others.

A clear example of a protected spirit is given in John 13:3, 4, where Jesus prepares to wash the disciples' feet before the Passover meal: "Jesus knew that the Father had put all things under his power, and that he had come from God and was returning to God; so he got up from the meal, took off his outer clothing, and wrapped a towel around his waist." Because He knew who He was and what His purpose was, He could wash the disciples' feet, knowing that Judas would betray Him, Peter would deny knowing Him, and others would desert Him for a time.

Following this model doesn't guarantee that we won't experience hurt feelings. Remember that when Jesus approached him, Peter at first refused to let Him wash his feet. (John 13:8) While Peter's rejection may have hurt Jesus' feelings, it did not deter Jesus from His purpose, nor destroy His spirit.

The wall of self-protection _we_ build through will power and spiritually damaging dispositions prevents us from being who God created us to be, whereas the shielding of our spirit by the Holy Spirit frees us to live the abundant life that Jesus promises. In other words, our self-protection becomes a prison, while the Holy Spirit's protection empowers and sets us free.

The shielding of our spirit by the Holy Spirit frees us to live the abundant life that Jesus promises.

Assignment
Awareness

1. Each of us has two voices that operate within our lives: the voice of hope and grace (Christ) and the voice of shame (Satan). Describe what the voice of hope would say to you today in all your circumstances and relationships.

2. Ask yourself daily, "What can I do today to remind myself that I am God's child?" The key word is "remind." We already are children of God, but we often forget. Look for ways to remind yourself of the identity that God has given you. This may come through friendships, Bible study, prayer, worship, support groups, nature, music, etc. <u>Write in your journal</u> what you discover about your identity in Christ.

3. Write yourself a letter of permission to be human. This is a recognition of your need and dependency on Christ rather than a dependence on your own performance or behavior.

Chapter 7
Obedience

"We demolish arguments and every pretension that sets itself up against the knowledge of God, and we take captive every thought to make it obedient to Christ." II Corinthians 10:5

After we become aware of our unmet needs, we are faced with a decision: Are we going to continue as before with our self- made protection around our spirits, or are we willing to allow the Holy Spirit to protect us?

All of us have wounded spirits as a result of living in an imperfect world where our experiences in life color our view of God, ourselves, and others — reshaping and warping truth for us. For example, if we are consistently rejected, our truth becomes, "We deserve to be rejected." As a result, we expect rejection as well, and that expectation pervades our thinking, feeling, and behavior.

One Sunday morning, I overheard a father warning his young daughter about the consequences of fidgeting and talking during the church service. He said to her, "If you don't sit still, God is going to get you." Then to add emphasis to his statement, he physically moved away from her, as if to say, "If God does get you, I want to be safely out of the way." This precious child will grow into a young adult who may intellectually understand God's grace, but will fail to experience it. In other words, her "gut feelings" as an adult will tell her that she must earn God's approval, for that's what her spirit experienced when she was a child.

Feelings and truth

We must listen to our feelings because they are reactions from our heart that communicate what needs healing in our spirit. Feelings of inadequacy, for example, point to an underlying wound that needs the application of God's truth and healing love. Our feelings are neither right nor wrong. They must be recognized and acknowledged because they are shaped by our experience. But since they don't necessarily reflect God's truth, our feelings must be examined in the light of that truth.

We must listen to our feelings because they are reactions from our heart that communicate what needs healing in our spirit.

If our son wakes up crying during the night, saying there are monsters under his bed, we might respond in one of these ways:

1. Tell him, "Quit crying and go back to sleep." (Refuse to acknowledge his feelings.)
2. Tell him, "That's scary. Maybe you'd feel better if you got in bed with me." (Validate his feelings, but ignore the truth.)
3. Tell him, "I'm sorry you're so frightened. Why don't we get your flashlight out and take a look. I think you'll find there's nothing under there but dust bunnies." (Acknowledge and validate his feelings as well as help him discover the truth.)

Obviously, the third response is the healthier choice. We must "parent" ourselves using this same approach — first acknowledging our feelings as being genuine, but then examining God's truth. In order for us to move from the reality of our experiences to the truth of God, we must be willing to learn what God says about us.

A willing spirit

Familiarity is a great comfort to us, even when it is painful. Regardless of the discomfort, we can somehow manage to cope with the predictable. But this approach to life keeps us locked in our pattern of spiritually damaging traits and blocks us from the fullness of life God intended us to have. To embrace what He would tell us about who we are, we must first be willing to allow God to be involved in the reeducation process. Only then are change, transformation, and the experience of grace possible.

The movie "Indiana Jones and the Last Crusade" provides us an example of a willing spirit. During one of the last scenes of the movie, Indiana Jones suddenly finds himself at the end of a path which drops off into a deep chasm. Behind him are the "bad guys." He is faced with the choice of literally stepping out in faith into the chasm (the unknown) or being overtaken by his pursuers. Jones takes the step of faith, and an invisible bridge safely carries him across to his goal: the Holy Grail.

It is important to note that Jones took the step of faith only because the "bad guys" were after him, not because of some great understanding about the magical properties of the chasm before him. In real life, we must step out in faith to escape our spiritual "bad guys," such as depression and shame. Like Indiana Jones we must have a willing spirit that enables us to step out in faith even when we don't have all the answers. It is the only way we will reach our goal: a life of peace, joy, and love.

A teachable spirit

Our natural inclination is to protect ourselves through control and knowing all the "right" answers and all the "right" ways to think, act, feel, and believe. A teachable spirit, on the other hand, surrenders to the Holy Spirit, relinquishes the need to control, and opens up to Christ's teachings. Even though these new truths feel scary and unnatural, we can be assured that we are now moving in the right direction by examining the teachings in light of the five elements that shape our spirit.

> Do they convey God's love, grace, and presence in our life?
> Do they increase our desire to be in fellowship with Christ and to seek His will?
> Do they increase our love for Jesus?
> Do they confirm our value and worth as revealed to us by Christ?
> Do they give us a clear picture of who God created us to be?
> Do they give us increased meaning and purpose for our lives?

An obedient spirit

Because our experiences serve as a language or means of " data entry" to our spirit, they shape how we see ourselves, God, and our world. In many ways, our sense of worth, meaning, and purpose, as well as the dynamics of our relationships with others, is heavily impacted by the full range of our experiences. For us to be willing to let Christ's love heal us and the Holy Spirit fill and protect us, there comes a point when all the talking is over, and it's time to step out in faith and obedience.

Our experiences serve as a language or means of "data entry" to our spirit.

This principle is wonderfully illustrated in Matthew's account of Jesus walking on the water. (Matthew 14: 22- 33) When Jesus asks Peter to step out of the boat and walk to Him on the water, Peter doesn't stop to discuss his doubts about himself or the improbability of being able to walk on water. Neither does the disciple say he needs to be a better person first, try harder, memorize more Scriptures, nor gain more wisdom to accept Christ's invitation. Regardless of his feelings about leaving the familiar environment of the boat, he simply steps out to join Christ on the churning surface of the sea.

As long as Peter looked at his Lord, he actually walked on the water toward Jesus. But when he took his eyes off Christ and looked at the frightening wind-blown sea about him, he began to sink, calling out, "Lord, save me!" Verse 31 says, "Immediately Jesus reached out his hand and caught him."

We, too, need Peter's initial faith that moved him beyond his feelings and the misgivings of experience to a step of obedience.

We, too, need Peter's initial faith that moved him beyond his feelings and the misgivings of experience to a step of obedience. If we wait for our feelings to change before we believe that God's love, grace, forgiveness, and healing apply to us, we will wait a lifetime, because our feelings are tied to our wounds. But if we respond in obedience to Christ's call, He will enable us to walk above what, in the past, has engulfed us — as long as we keep our eyes fixed on Him. And because of His grace, He will catch us if we call out to Him when we feel ourselves falling back into hopelessness and despair.

There's another story about Peter that demonstrates the response of obedience without regard to previous experience. This one, found in John 21:1-14,

Scripture Journaling

"Your word is a lamp to my feet and a light for my path." Psalm 119:105

Do you believe God's word is a lamp for your feet? Maybe you do, but you're not too sure that your path is very well lit at all! Scripture journaling is all about <u>your feelings</u> in regard to passages from the Bible.

takes place after Christ's resurrection. Following a whole night of fishing in which not a single fish was caught, Peter and six other disciples are returning in their empty boat. Christ (whom they do not yet recognize) calls out from the shore, telling them that if they throw their nets on the right side of the boat, they will catch fish. Remember, now, that Peter is not a casual fisherman, but one who relies on fishing to support his family. Not only is he familiar with the feeding habits of fish, but he knows the best locations and times when the right combination of tides and weather conditions should result in catching fish.

The Scripture passage does not give us clues as to why Peter chose to respond to the instruction of the stranger on the shore. Perhaps it was out of desperation for the income that a good catch of fish would bring. Or maybe he was thinking, "What have I got to lose?" Whatever the reason, Peter <u>ignored</u> the gut-level certainty of the fish-less <u>experience</u> of the last several hours and obeyed Christ's command, ordering the net thrown over the right side of the boat. His obedience resulted in a net so full of fish that it could not be hauled in and had to be towed to shore instead.

Christ stands on the shore calling to us as well, telling us to cast out in obedience and faith that He alone will provide nourishment for our spirit. Only when we ignore the false "wisdom" of our past experience and take the first step of obedience — because He says we are worthy — will we begin to move toward the grace that will bring us healing and wholeness. Like Peter, our first act of obedience may be driven by desperation or a what-have-I-got-to-lose attitude. Nevertheless, when we see God's bountiful response to our obedience, we will become deeply convinced that His plan for us is perfect.

Taking the risk

When we are willing to be taught, willing to do whatever it takes, and willing to risk being changed, God will bless our efforts and begin to do a work of healing and transformation in us. The final results — the how and the when of healing — are up to God, but we must be willing to go where He leads us. In essence, we must allow God to direct our healing according to His plan. While He may choose to heal us differently than we had hoped or prayed, we can risk obeying God because we can trust our loving Heavenly Father's heart.

When we are willing to be taught, willing to do whatever it takes, and willing to risk being changed, God will bless our efforts and begin to do a work of healing and transformation in us.

Dennis was distraught when his wife moved out of their home while she confronted a lot of pain and confusion about her past. Knowing that the soundness and health of his marriage was very poor, he came to me for counsel. Not only was he willing to give his wife time for healing, but he also recognized his part in their marriage problems and decided to address his own wounds and spiritually damaging dispositions and traits. Dennis eagerly worked on the assignments I gave him and sought the support of other Christian friends to pray for him. Without any assurance that his marriage would be salvaged, he took the risk of letting God change and heal him.

Operating only on the basis of our feelings and experience, we will remain locked in place. But if we shift our gaze from our fear of the known and the unknown and look instead to Christ, we can take the path of healing. The only requirements for the journey are a willing, teachable spirit and enough faith to risk taking the first step of obedience. Trusting that the Holy Spirit will protect us, we can shed our self-made armor and put ourselves in the hands of the Great Physician. Are you ready?

Assignment
Obedience

1. Pray for a softening of your heart to recognize God's presence.

2. Ask God to insulate your spirit for (a) protection, (b) healing, and (c) growth.

3. <u>Keep a Scripture journal</u>. If, for instance, your unmet need is value, use a Bible concordance to look up the word value as well as its synonyms, such as importance, significance, grace, and honor. Look up these Scriptures and do the following four things:

   (a) Memorize the Scripture.

   (b) Write what the Scripture feels like to you, e.g., "This is hard for me to believe. I have doubts. It gives me hope. It gives me a sense of peace, etc." Be honest. Let your Scriptural journaling reflect your honest feelings (positive or negative), not your intellectual understanding. Remember that feelings are reactions from the heart that will help you identify your wounds. This is not the time to describe your intellectual understanding or identify life application principles. [Example: "God may forgive others, but I don't believe this applies to me. I feel sad that this is not in my life," or "God's forgiveness is very comforting and reassuring."]

   (c) Share your Scripture and journaling with another person in order to receive his or her understanding of both the Scripture and you.

   (d) Pray. Let your prayer be a direct result of your journaling. If you write that you have doubts, then your prayer should ask for faith, understanding, or insight. If you write that you feel peace, then you should say a prayer of thanksgiving. [Example: "Help me to be aware of your forgiveness even if I don't feel it now."]

Note: See the next page for additional assistance on this very important assignment.

Scripture Journaling

It can be hard to get started with Scripture journaling. For some people, it's even more difficult to keep from getting carried away. Don't be tempted to take shortcuts or to preach or to ignore the parts that make you uncomfortable. And don't "stretch the truth," even a little bit.

Remember that Scripture journaling is all about feelings — your feelings — as you read God's word. It is your feelings that will reveal the wounds to your spirit. Don't lose sight of your goal to set down genuine, honest, gut-level feelings. For if you become evasive or flowery, you'll miss the whole point of the exercise.

Here are some guidelines to help you get started:

I. Do as many as you are comfortable with every week -- one a day, several a week, or as often as possible.

II. You can do it alone, but there are benefits to working with a partner. We <u>all</u> have wounds! Not only does a partner hold you accountable, it's always nice to have their intercessory prayer. Ask them to pray for your understanding of the Scripture as it applies to you.

III. Select a portion of Scripture from those listed in Appendix A. Verses may be typed by subject matter and cut apart for ready use, or simply hand written.

IV. Memorize the verse or commit it to a good understanding.

V. Write in your journal about the Scripture passage. Approach your writing from one of the following:

    A. I agree with the verse(s).
       1. Why?
       2. Elaborate briefly.
       3. Pray or write a prayer. (Example: "I claim this Scripture for my life. I claim God's truth about ______ for my life. Thank you, God, for ______.")

    B. I disagree with the verse(s).
       1. Why? (Example: "I see this in other people's lives but not in mine; I don't understand why ______; This bothers me because ______; It makes me feel angry, guilty, etc.; God wouldn't/doesn't feel that way about me, etc.)
       2. Elaborate briefly.
       3. If you recognize a wound at this point, acknowledge it.
       4. Pray or write a prayer. (Example: "Here's the wound, Lord. . . . ; I don't believe/understand/wasn't aware of this, etc.; Open my eyes to this today. Help me to see your value/love/etc. of me, or to see the wound, or to experience Your comfort. Open my eyes to Your presence in my life. Grant me a greater portion of Your ______ today. Comfort me, Lord, when others ______ or when I feel ______. Pour Your ______ and ______ into my life as I struggle to deal with ______."

VI. Remember: Christ is the only one who can fully heal your woundedness. It is critical that you know and trust that He has felt everything you are, or ever will be, struggling with.

Chapter 8
Transformation

"Do not conform any longer to the pattern of this world,
but be transformed by the renewing of your mind.
Then you will be able to test and approve what
God's will is — his good, pleasing and perfect will."
Romans 12:2

Oftentimes, we try to "fix" our problem by deciding to make some changes. We quit crying and complaining, or we try to behave more lovingly toward our spouse, for example. We may also work on thinking positively and changing our outlook on life. We're not only going to act "normal," we're going to make ourselves think as though "everything is just great!" We may even make attempts to arbitrarily change our feelings about the person or situation.

Books and counseling may give us insights about why we are the way we are and "labels" to put on ourselves and our situation. But the understanding that comes from these insights and labels does not heal us; it only confirms our need for God's healing touch.

The understanding that comes from these insights and labels does not heal us; it only confirms our need for God's healing touch.

The concept of "self-help" is flawed because it is based on the false assumption that we can heal ourselves through the control of our will. While these measures may result in some measure of relief, the improvement is only short-term because it is circumstantial. The mental, emotional, and physical exhaustion of our efforts or even a slight shift in our circumstances can defeat us.

Changing our actions, beliefs, and feelings <u>are</u> steps in the recovery process, but <u>only</u> if these changes grow out of a new attitude that reflects God's truth and are empowered by Him. True, lasting change and healing result, not from will power, but from God's enabling as we surrender our will to His and begin to deal with the wounds of our spirit that underlie our pain and brokenness. Since these wounds are the result of sin, our human will is completely powerless to overcome them. We must also deal with our spiritually damaging dispositions and traits by which we try to deal with our woundedness instead of turning to God for deliverance and healing.

True, lasting change and healing result, not from will power, but from God's enabling as we surrender our will to His.

Transformation — taking what was broken and wounded and turning it into something whole and healed — is a work of God that begins with our inviting Him to do the work. Just as the first step in every 12-step recovery program acknowledges that we are powerless over our problem, the first step in our recovery begins with our acknowledgment that we have no power to heal ourselves, but that Christ is, indeed, the Great Physician.

Three-part transformation

All too often, our only thought is that we obtain relief, and so we ask God to heal us. After all, He is our Healer. But God is so much more: He is the Creator and Re-creator. Before the transformation of our lives can take place, we must experience cleansing and filling as well as healing. There are no short cuts.

Cleansing - a step of faith
Our sins and the strongholds of our spiritually damaging attitudes must be cleansed. This requires a step of faith as we express our confidence in the cleansing power of the blood of our Savior.

Filling - a step of obedience
In addition, we must fill our mind and spirit with God's truth, grace, and forgiveness. Since we may not, at first, feel that we have these blessings from God, this requires a step of obedience.

Healing - a step of vulnerability
The healing of our wounds requires a step of vulnerability as we allow God to comfort us. It is in the comfort of His love that our spirit is restored to wholeness.

As we will see in the next chapter, the order of these three steps may vary from person to person (and from time to time for the same person), but the essential truth remains: all three components are essential to our healing and transformation.

Cleansing through confession and repentance

Lisa, whose teenage son was in a drug treatment program, sat across from me weeping. "I'm a bad mother," she told me. "I hated the things I heard coming out of my mouth, but I couldn't stop myself. Why couldn't I have been more encouraging? Why didn't I listen more and scream less?"

Lisa had made some mistakes as a parent, and she recognized that fact. But facing the truth about ourselves should be a stepping stone to healing, not a trap door to shame. God want us to move from the pain of our recognized shortcomings and failings toward confession and repentance, and the grace, mercy, and forgiveness that He offers us.

Not only are we called to confess sinful acts, we must confess and repent of our spiritually damaging dispositions and traits because they mar the image of Christ in us. True repentance does not mean feeling guilty, doing penance, or merely "feeling sorry" about our sins. It is, rather, "turning God-ward," in a willingness to be transformed by the Holy Spirit. The sole purpose of our guilt is to make us aware of our dependence on Christ.

Although Nancy's ministry to women had been helpful to others, she suddenly quit and withdrew from her church family. When she came to see me, she was anxious, depressed, and experiencing "burnout." She talked about having realized that her ministry had been driven by a sense of duty. Looking back on her childhood, she began to see that she had learned early the necessity to "be perfect" in order to be loved and accepted.

Then one day Nancy poured out her shame about her "family secret," that her son was an abusive alcoholic. Only then was she able to see that she had allowed her shame and fear of being discovered to drive her from her ministry. With a sincere, repentant heart, she confessed her shame, fear, pride, control, and unforgiveness and received cleansing and healing. As a result, the Holy Spirit enabled Nancy to minister out of the fullness of God's grace instead of the need to perform.

We must be willing to shed the security of our spiritually damaging dispositions because they reinforce the lies and incorrect beliefs we hold on to. For example, if we have the attitude of fear, we retreat when opportunities come our way rather than take risks. Then shame attacks us, saying, "See, you can't do anything." Our fear prevents us from experiencing success, and our shame convinces us that success is not possible. Since we are never perfectly without these unhealthy attitudes and react from them almost automatically when we feel threatened or stressed, we need to cleanse our spirits each time we fall prey to them.

Antidotes for harmful dispositions

When we become aware of our spiritually damaging attitudes, not only can we find forgiveness through Christ, but we can also ask Him to develop in us a pleasing attitude that serves as an antidote. The following chart lists antidotes for each of our destructive dispositions.

Damaging Disposition	Antidote
shame	grace
control	faith
fear	gratitude
pride	worship
self-centeredness	humility
judgmentalism	thankfulness
resentment/bitterness	forgiveness
dishonesty	truth

If we easily fall prey to an attitude of fear, we need to exercise our gratitude "muscle" by reflecting each day on the things for which we can be thankful. To counteract our tendency toward shame, we can begin each day by reciting Biblical affirmations about who we are in Christ. And there's nothing quite like spending time in worship and adoration of our awesome God to tame our pride.

Sanctification

The removal of our spiritually damaging dispositions points us toward wholeness through the work of sanctification. This is a different process than conversion. Our conversion makes us new creatures in Christ because it brings us forgiveness, a new identity, and restored fellowship with Christ. But even after conversion, the strongholds of our destructive attitudes are still present. In the process of sanctification, we keep moving toward perfection as Christ commanded us. Although we will never be without flaw, our goal is to grow ever closer to the pattern of Christ's perfect love and His dependence on God.

The verse in Romans cited at the beginning of this chapter urges us to be transformed by the renewing of our mind so that we no longer conform to the pattern of this world. (12:2) The Latin root of the word conform means "to be shaped after." Since our spiritually damaging dispositions and traits are shaped by our self-protective response to our woundedness, being cleansed and released from them will free us for being reshaped into greater Christlikeness. That reshaping is the process of sanctification.

During this process, which continues throughout our lifetime, Christ's transforming hand upon us frees us for the production of spiritual fruit: love, joy, peace, patience, kindness, goodness, faithfulness, gentleness, and self-control. (Galatians 5:22-23)

Change me!

Many, many times, people come to me for counseling and, after telling me about the difficulties they are experiencing in their lives, they ask for my help in changing them — as if I could! Basically, we _do_ want to be different: to treat others better, to react to crises with calm instead of panic, to not feel such anger and resentment toward people and situations that hurt us. But instead of asking God to make us who _we_ want to be, though, our prayer should be: "Lord, make me who _You_ created me to be!"

In changing us, God does not give us a personality "make- over," where the old us is thrown out and He starts all over with us from scratch. Rather, He cleans us up and puts our personality characteristics under the transforming leadership of the Holy Spirit. Our stubbornness can be tempered into persistence and tenacity; our hypersensitivity can be molded into empathy and the gift of mercy. There is no end to His creativity, for even our limitations can be used to bless us and others.

God is the Master Craftsman weaving the parts of our lives together in a way that brings Him glory and serves to build His kingdom. Even when we don't feel His presence, He is ever at work to bring us to wholeness in Himself. We often struggle because we are an impatient people, driven by clocks and calendars, while God works according to His own perfect timing. We must stand in the confidence that He is never too late!

Being cleansed and released from our spiritually damaging dispositions and traits will free us for being reshaped into greater Christlikeness.

The Great Physician

Healing seems elusive until we bring our wounds and spiritually damaging dispositions and traits to the cross of Christ for cleansing and comfort. For, much as in a fog, we cannot see the necessity of Christ's involvement. Until then, there can be no true healing.

Assignment
Transformation

1. Review your answers to the assignment at the end of Chapter 5, "Self-inflicted Spiritual Damage," and reflect on the state of your spirit. Identify other traits and dispositions that you now recognize as being sinful.

2. Through prayer, confess all of your spiritually damaging, sinful attitudes to God, and ask Him for forgiveness. Also, ask God to cleanse these traits and dispositions from your life, to empower you with Christ-like attitudes, and to transform you into His likeness.

3. Visualize God pouring His grace and strength into you. You do <u>not</u> have to try to conjure them up from within yourself.

Chapter 9
Path to Healing

*"You have made known to me the path of life; you will
fill me with joy in your presence, with eternal pleasures
at your right hand."* Psalm 16:11

Generally speaking, we seek professional counseling when we are in turmoil
or feel our life is out of control. Sensing that we've lost our grip and struggling
to cope or even to survive, we send up a flare that acknowledges we're in
trouble. The recognizable factors in our suffering usually fall into these four
categories:

- an event - such as death, divorce, illness, job loss, "empty
  nest," physical or sexual assault, etc.
- emotions and negative thinking - such as depression, anxiety,
  being critical, inability to be happy, etc.
- behaviors - such as adultery or other marital problems,
  difficulties with children, etc.
- addictions - ours or someone else's

Regardless of the fact that we have no idea that our discomfort stems from
our destructive attitudes and unmet spiritual needs, we have taken the first
step toward healing by acknowledging that we have a problem.

Healing God's way and in His time
When we ask God to be in charge of our healing, He brings about healing
according to His will and His timing. Sometimes, He heals us <u>instantly</u>.
Many references in the Scriptures show Christ restoring sight to the blind,
making the lame walk, cleansing lepers, and raising the dead to life with
only the touch of His hand. When He chooses to do so, God still heals that
way. It has been my experience, though, that God most often restores our
wholeness through a <u>healing process</u> in which He heals us layer by layer.
Because deeper healing is needed at some level, the process may be made up
of numerous individual healing steps interspersed by periods of further
learning, cleansing, and greater filling with His Spirit. While we are usually
in a hurry to "get on with it," we must learn to trust His knowledge of all that
remains to be healed, as well as His greater purpose to be achieved in our
lives.

*God most often restores
our wholeness through a
<u>healing process</u> in which
He heals us layer
by layer.*

Paul's teaching on his "thorn in the flesh" (II Corinthians 12:7-10) indicates another way that God heals: by <u>enabling us to endure our suffering</u> through complete reliance on His sufficiency to meet our needs. Despite the fact that Paul asked God three times to take away the "thorn" (whatever it was), He refused. God saw that more could be achieved through Paul's continued suffering than would be accomplished by relieving his pain. Paul's strength to endure through God's enabling is a concept of healing that may not line up with our expectations or understanding about healing. But the fact that Paul's "thorn" did not defeat him or hamper his effectiveness in ministry indicates that he received some dimension of healing grace.

We must be careful not to assume that it's God's will if our suffering continues. It may be that we are being disobedient in something God calls us to do in order to further the process of our healing, such as additional forgiveness work or making amends. At the same time, we must not automatically assume that our suffering means we've done something wrong. We must seek God in prayer — and ask others to intercede for us as well — in order to discern God's will.

Sometimes God's method of healing us is through a <u>process that requires greater spiritual and/or emotional maturity</u>. In essence, our healing will not be complete until we do some more growing up. God may deliver us of our spiritually damaging attitude of fear, for example, yet we must learn to live by faith in order to be fully healed. Rather than plugging into an instant supply, we acquire faith through practice — by learning to trust God in increasingly greater degrees. Our progress may be measured in baby steps as we develop the tools necessary to function at a greater level of maturity. Like the athlete who has trouble walking after the surgical correction of a torn knee ligament, we may question whether our problem has been "fixed." But just as his assurance of full recovery increases as he exercises to develop greater physical strength, our confidence in our healing will increase as we develop greater spiritual and emotional strength.

No matter which method God uses, we can trust His judgment in tailoring our healing to fulfill all that He wants to accomplish, resting in the confidence that with Him we can endure anything because His provision for us is sufficient. God gives us His anointing for the healing process, flooding us with His love, grace, and strength to empower our transformation into spiritual wholeness. As a result, we can be vulnerable to His healing touch, trusting in His method and timing, instead of telling Him how and when to heal us.

Above and below the surface

In addition to what we remember about our past, there are also memories that lie below the level of our consciousness. Whether remembered or deeply hidden in our subconscious, many events and circumstances result in our believing something about ourselves that is simply not true. This is the <u>core lie</u> that we believe: "<u>Because it happened, I caused it. It's my fault.</u>" From this lie springs our <u>core shame</u>: "<u>Therefore, I am bad, unloved, insignificant, etc.</u>" These are the beliefs that you have about yourself because of the

We can be vulnerable to God's healing touch, trusting in His method and timing, instead of telling Him how and when to heal us.

The Smoke Bomb

Imagine that someone throws a smoke bomb into the room where you are sitting. Billows of thick smoke fill the room, causing you to cough and gasp for air. Instinctively, you close your eyes. At some point, the flow of smoke stops. You don't know whether someone removed the smoke bomb or it simply emptied. Nevertheless, since the room remains smoky, you continue to keep your eyes tightly shut. Your nose still burns, and you're coughing repeatedly.

The throwing of the smoke bomb represents some event that wounded your spirit. You can't do anything about it; it's in the past. Nevertheless, you must deal with the consequences of the event — the room full of smoke. The inflammation of your eyes, nose, and throat caused by the smoke represents the wounds to your spirit.

You try to cope by keeping your eyes shut and putting a handkerchief over your mouth and nose. Despite these attempts at self-protection, you continue to get hurt as you stumble around the room bumping into things. And because of your anger and unforgiveness toward the one who threw the smoke bomb, you find it hard to trust that someone will help you. (You don't recognize that your spiritually damaging dispositions are adding to your misery.)

throwing of the smoke bomb .... **event**

room full of smoke .... **consequences**

irritation of eyes, nose, throat .... **wounds to the spirit**

shutting eyes, covering nose & mouth .... **self-protection**

coping through pride/control .... **destructive attitude**

safety, security, value .... **unmet needs of the spirit**

The only beneficial course is to deal with the effects of the smoke bomb and the resulting damage by opening a window (seeking healing) to let in some fresh air (God's truth). Don't forget: Healing isn't complete until you forgive the person who threw the smoke bomb!

wounding of your spirit.

On the conscious level, we are filled with fear, anxiety, and panic. A <u>secondary lie</u> develops as we try to escape our discomfort by deciding, "<u>I must be perfect. I must be in control</u>." Hiding our true self behind a mask, we present ourselves as we think others should see us. We develop spiritually damaging dispositions and traits as a means of protecting ourselves from further discomfort, as well as addictions to numb our pain. These are the only ways we know to cope with our underlying brokenness; following God's plan never occurs to us.

But when we do turn to God instead of trying to maintain control, the core lie we believed is replaced by <u>core truth</u>: "<u>Because it happened, it hurt</u>." Once we admit our pain we can grieve our loss, which is what we've been avoiding because we were afraid of the pain. The God-ordained process of grieving will result in the replacing of our core shame with <u>core grace</u>: "<u>God will bring healing through this process</u>."

Where was God?

When we do remember times of intense pain and suffering, this question comes all too quickly to our lips: "Where was God when . . . ?" Our understanding of a loving Heavenly Father is shaken by what we perceive of as His abandonment in our greatest hour of need. The truth is that God was right beside us: feeling our pain, grieving for our suffering, and teaching us how to survive by creating within us the ability to protect ourselves. True, these survival techniques may result in spiritually destructive attitudes which must be cleansed and transformed. But we can come to grips with this apparent contradiction if we keep in mind that God never says, "Ooops, shouldn't have done that!" God never makes mistakes and He never acts contrary to His character. "And we know that in all things God works for the good of those who love him, who have been called according to his purpose." (Romans 8:28)

"Hitting bottom"

In the field of alcohol treatment, counselors once embraced the idea that alcoholics must "hit bottom" before they would be ready to receive help. However, we now recognize that it is too risky to wait for the "bottom." Instead, we create a crisis that feels like the bottom because the alcoholic discovers the coping devices that worked in the past don't work anymore. Once their options are gone, alcoholics can begin to understand their need for help.

In the same way, we often need a crisis in our lives to bring us to the point where we must acknowledge our dependence on Christ and His truth. Without this feeling of helplessness and despair, we, too, cling to our control options, which often begin in our thoughts as: "If I just . . . then . . . " The bottom feels like failure and defeat, but in reality it is the place of vulnerable surrender to the One who can truly lift us up. For instead of falling to the bottom of a chasm, we are falling into God's loving, healing hands. This is actually the point where we can face our deepest hurts and shame because it is where we are met by God's gifts of grace and love. The gifts may not make sense to us; we only know that we desperately need them.

Healing from inside out or outside in

In most cases, we heal from the inside out, by dealing first with the wounds to our spirit. Although our spiritual health is deeply affected by our spiritually damaging dispositions and traits, we are better able to confess and repent of these self-destructive tendencies after the wounds from which they grew are cleansed and healed. Then, when we don't need these harmful attitudes any more, we can willingly and more easily give them up. It's as though we can throw away our misshaped crutch — which only further hampered our walk — once our initial lameness is healed. But we may also exhibit attitudes that are so deeply entrenched that our spirits are encrusted and we cannot see our wound. We must strip away these sinful responses to our pain before looking below to the underlying woundedness.

Release from our spiritually damaging attitudes requires true repentance, for we must recognize them as sin. If, for example, we endeavor to overcome our unforgiveness and quick temper by trying to quit being resentful, we have just created a new sinful attitude of control. And when we fail, we will probably create another damaging way of thinking — that of shame.

We tend to return to our dominant sinful inclination when we are placed under stress or experience further wounding. The good news is that we do not need to worry about, or struggle with, our spiritually damaging attitudes on a daily basis. Through Christ, we can be released from them and become a living witness to God's power to heal. Why would we doubt Christ's ability to remove such feelings as fear, shame, and unforgiveness when He was able to raise Lazarus from the dead?

The path to healing

The list below describes the stepping stones along the path to healing.
- embracing God's truth in faith
- illumination
- confession and repentance
- grief work
- accepting God's grace
- forgiveness work
- overcoming oppression
- amends work
- continued spiritual growth
- sharing our healing

As healing progresses, our path may climb a steady slope or spiral upward as we have to circle back to repeat some step. At other times, we may get stuck along the way as we look away from God. But regardless of the "terrain" and our "spiritual fitness," we can be confident that our loving Companion is at our side to encourage and empower our next step.

In most cases, we heal from the inside out, by dealing first with the wounds to our spirit.

But we may also exhibit attitudes that are so deeply entrenched that our spirits are encrusted and we cannot see our wound.

Falling into God's Loving Hands

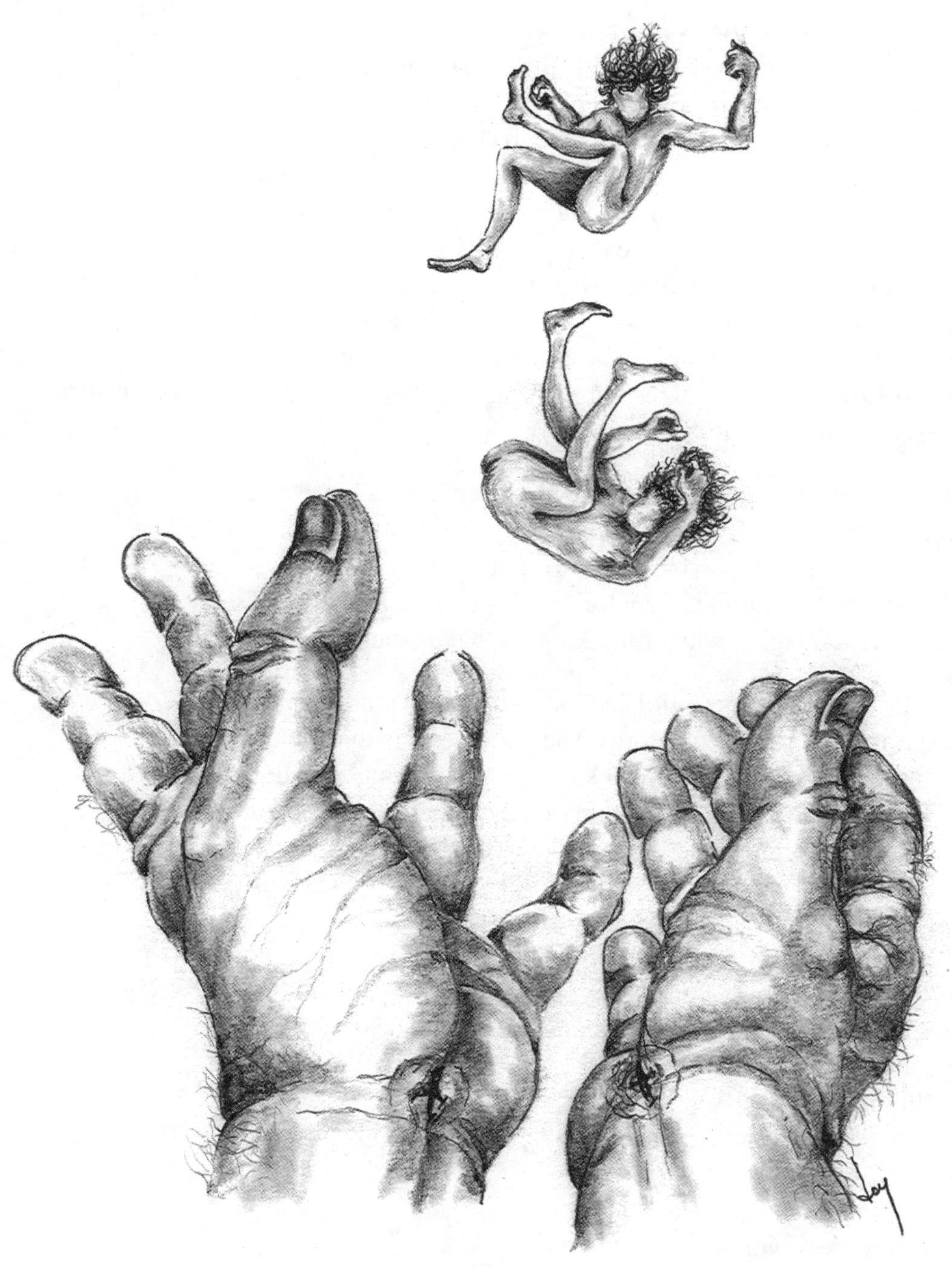

It usually takes a crisis to begin the healing process. Unable to heal ourselves and feeling angry, hurt, ashamed, unloved, and helpless, we face our greatest fear of all: rejection. In despair, we finally "let go" and begin what seems like a free fall into the dark unknown. But instead of falling into a bottomless chasm, we find that we are falling into the loving, healing hands of God!

Assignment
Path to Healing

This exercise is a "Grief Grid" to help you record your progress in the healing process. Date the steps as you continue working your way through the book and complete the grief and healing work involved. You may want to put the information on a chart or use a page in your journal for each part of the exercise. Since some of these steps are assignments in other chapters, feel free to abbreviate your responses for this exercise. Take encouragement from the progress you are making.

Event - What caused your wound?

Feelings - What feelings do you associate with that event?

Beliefs - What lies did you believe about yourself, others, and God as a result of the event and your feelings? Replace them with God's truths about you.

Wounds - How was your spirit wounded by the event? (What needs of your spirit were not met?)

Sinful Attitudes - How have you tried to compensate for your woundedness and protect yourself from further pain? Note the date of your prayers of confession and repentance.

Forgiveness - Whom do you need to forgive? Place the date beside each name as you forgive them. Did you remember to include yourself as well as God?

Gifts from the Wounds - How has God gifted you for ministry to others because of your own experience? Express your gratitude for your gifts.

Chapter 10
Truth

"Show me your ways, O Lord, teach me your paths; guide me in your truth and teach me, for you are God my Savior, and my hope is in you all day long." Psalm 25:4-5

In our journey through the healing process, we must learn to recognize the misconceptions about ourselves that we pick up through our life experiences. If, for example, someone has told us over and over again that we are stupid, the focus of forgiveness is really about forgiving the person for making us believe something that isn't true. Through forgiving the individual we claim the belief in our own worth or value.

Moving from our misconceptions about our self (and life) toward truth is a difficult journey. It is a journey of faith in which we let go of our negative experiences in order to claim God's truth, replacing the lies we have believed with the truth as God declares it to be. In order to move toward wholeness, we must claim some basic truths — not because we feel them or even believe them, but because God has revealed them to us through Christ. This truly requires a journey of faith.

We must claim some basic truths — not because we feel them or even believe them, but because God has revealed them to us through Christ.

Living "up" to the lies
Neal's marriage was breaking apart. When I asked him if he knew why, he admitted to having had a series of affairs. "I think I'm addicted to sex," he told me. Neal sincerely wanted to salvage his relationship with his wife, Gayle, and did not take his infidelity lightly. "I feel terrible afterwards because I really do love Gayle. Why do I continue doing something that only makes me feel worse and worse?"

An examination of his past revealed that Neal's father, a minister, was demanding and perfectionistic. His mother, who was careful to keep up a good front (especially around people in the church), was an angry woman who vented her rage on her sons. As a result, Neal had become a victim of religious and spiritual abuse. He was convinced that he was not just bad, but evil, and that there was something defective about him. As an adult, he had been living "up" to those lies while seeking to numb the pain in his spirit through sexual gratification.

"God's Truth 101"

These seven truths are foundational. Through them, our spirit can safely begin shedding its crusting of self-protection and move toward an open attitude of hopeful expectancy.

1. **God loves us.** - God created us to be in a love relationship with Him. He loves each of us as unique individuals and wants to be in fellowship with us. Our worth and value are rooted in our being His beloved child.

2. **God forgives us.** - God forgives us no matter what we do — or don't do — because it is His nature to forgive. Although we will <u>never</u> deserve His forgiveness, all we have to do is acknowledge our sin, repent, and ask for His forgiveness. It is not something we can earn. His grace is sufficient.

3. **God will bring restoration.** - God always has the last word. We often feel overwhelmed by our circumstances, but God promises restoration for our losses. It may not be in terms we can see or understand, but God will heal our wounds and make us whole.

4. **God never leaves us or forsakes us.** - God is present in all the circumstances of our lives. Many times we feel abandoned by God because we do not understand, nor feel, His presence. God's presence with us is a fact; it is not a feeling. Our human feelings and limited understanding do not change that fact.

5. **God transforms us.** - God takes our personalities and transforms them for His purpose. We often give up on ourselves because of what we see as negative. But if we place our whole personality under God's guidance, He will transform our weaknesses and increase our strengths.

6. **God meets all of our spiritual needs.** - God designed us with spiritual needs, and His plan is to fill our emptiness. He yearns to fulfill our needs and restore us to wholeness. When people and situations have left holes in our spirits, Christ is there to fill them.

7. **God has meaning and purpose for us.** - God entrusts us with talents and abilities because He has a meaning and purpose for each of us. A recognition that God has a purpose for our lives inspires us and creates enthusiasm within us.

In therapy, Neal examined the lies about himself that were fostered in his early years and began to look at the truths of God in terms of his value and worth. Gayle, who wanted to save the marriage because of their young son, came with Neal to many counseling sessions. In the end, Neal's self-concept and his attitude about life in general were transformed by God's truth. Not only was his marriage healed, but Neal also began to minister as a lay person to men who struggle with sexual addiction.

Attitude adjustment

Our attitude reflects the state of our spirit, for it is the posture from which we approach life. As we saw in Chapter 5, we exhibit spiritually damaging dispositions and traits as a means of compensating for our spiritual woundedness or of protecting ourselves from further wounding. When we begin to accept God's truth on faith as the first step to healing our spirit, the need for the old turtle shell of self-protection is no longer necessary. We can then ask God to forgive and cleanse these attitudes of shame, fear, bitterness and resentment, denial and dishonesty, pride and control, judgmentalism and critical spirit, self-centeredness, and unforgiveness.

Our attitude reflects the state of our spirits, for it is the posture from which we approach life.

As a result, our attitude will be transformed and healed by God's grace. We will become increasingly aware that no person or situation has the ability to destroy our worth and value in God's eyes; to destroy God's love for us; to change our relationship with Christ; or to destroy the person God created us to be.

The belt of truth

Once we begin to cast off our self-protective covering, we must put on God's protection for our spirit. This armor of God is described in Ephesians 6:10-18. A critically important element of this armor, the belt of truth serves as a boundary around our spirit. It results in a truth-based, God-focused outlook, reflecting our understanding that His grace is constantly at work in our lives, regardless of our circumstances. When we acknowledge His love and presence, it makes all the difference in the world in how we think, act, react, and feel, and enables us to "run and not grow weary, . . . walk and not be faint." (Isaiah 40:31)

The belt of truth serves as a boundary around our spirit.

Stages of recovery

Accepting God's truth is an act of faith; it is not based on a sense of belief nor a strong feeling. Since our feelings are tied to our experiences, we cannot wait until we "feel" these things; otherwise we will never embrace these truths. Look at the chart on the following page, which outlines the stages of recovery.

Stages of Recovery

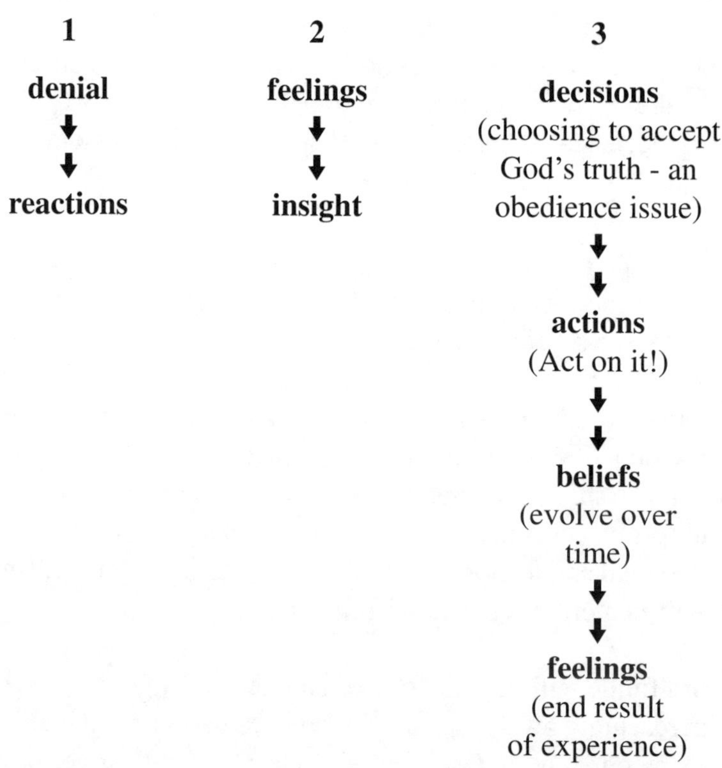

In stage one, we are unaware of our issues (the damaging events that caused our spiritual wounds), but we realize that our reactions are out of balance with the situation. If someone cuts in front of us on the freeway, for instance, we become extremely angry, blowing our horn, driving up close behind them, or aggressively cutting them (or someone else) off at the first opportunity. Or we may simply burst into tears. Although we sense that we are more angry, hurt, or fearful than present circumstances warrant, we deny that there is a deeper level to our discomfort.

Although we sense that we are more angry, hurt, or fearful than present circumstances warrant, we deny that there is a deeper level to our discomfort.

In stage two, our feelings lead to insight: "Aha! The reason I feel hurt is because this reminds me of the hurt I felt when . . ." For example, when a rude salesperson makes us feel slighted by ignoring us and helping the attractive customer who just walked up to the counter, we may realize that we have never felt that our needs mattered. But instead of leading us to healing, the insight just becomes additional evidence that we don't have value.

Instead of leading us to healing, the insight just becomes additional evidence that we don't have value.

Many of us are stuck in the denial/reactions stage. And although some of us may gain more insight and understanding from time to time, we never move toward wholeness, remaining instead a victim to our past.

Stage three requires a decision of faith — a decision to embrace the seven God-ordained truths, even though we may not, at first, feel them or believe them. For only when we decide to accept God's truth about who He is and who we are in Him can we expect real change and real healing, for His truth serves as our foundation for life, our guiding light, and the encircling protection for our spirit.

Then we begin to act in ways that reflect these decisions. I'm not talking about deciding to arbitrarily change the way we act based on our own will and driven by sheer determination. That's "self-help," and it will never last. I am saying that we can act differently in our response to life because we have decided to operate under the assumption that what God's word says about Him and us is true. And since God created us to live this way, He will empower us to act in ways that reflect His truth. It is only then that our beliefs about ourselves and our sufficiency in Christ begin to be transformed by the light of God's truth. Finally, a new set of feelings will evolve as true healing takes place.

Will you step out to make your decision of faith in Christ and His ability to heal you?

His truth serves as our foundation for life, our guiding light, and the encircling protection for our spirit.

We can act differently in our response to life because we have decided to operate under the assumption that what God's word says about Him and us is true.

Until we accept God's truth . . .

This maze illustrates the first two stages of recovery. Initially, we may be in denial of having any spiritual wounds, but we realize that our reactions to situations are off-balance. In the next stage, our feelings lead us to insight as to the *cause* of our discomfort. But instead of leading us to healing, the insight just becomes additional evidence that we are, somehow, defective. Many of us continue to cycle back and forth between these two stages and never move toward healing and wholeness.

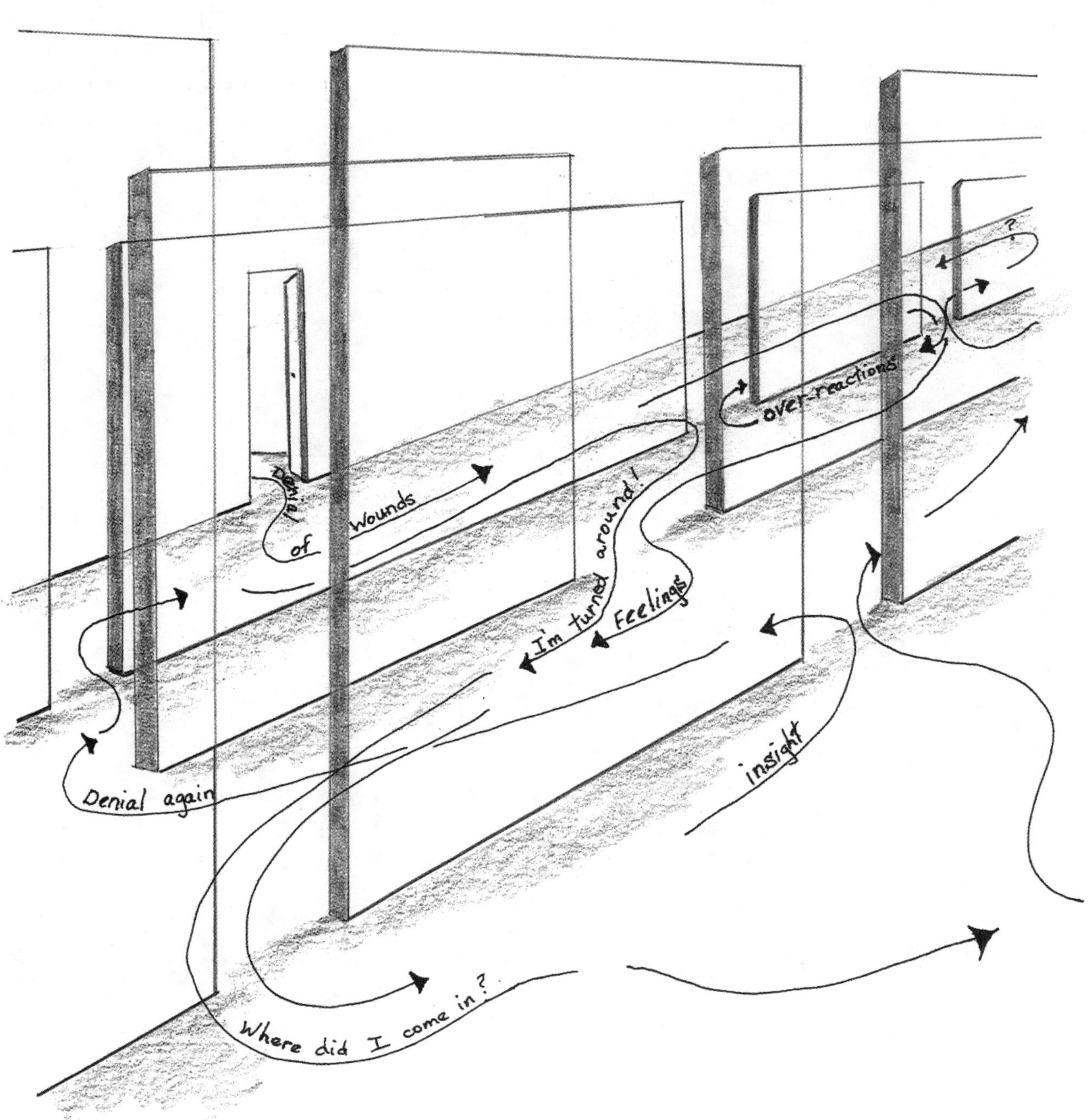

The final stage of recovery begins with a decision to accept God's truths on faith — even though we may not, at first, feel them or truly believe them. Then we need to follow up that step of obedience by acting on the basis of God's truth. In time, our beliefs about ourselves and our sufficiency in Christ will be transformed by the light of that truth. New feelings will grow out of the realization of our new identity.

Don't let a "brick wall" stop your healing. Climb out of the maze and move into a richer, fuller life in Christ.

Assignment
Truth

1. On a sheet of paper, list the lies that you have accepted regarding God, self, others, and relationships. These are wrong beliefs that you may not believe intellectually, but that you automatically adhere to in your life. These beliefs are generally absolutes with little room for the gray. Examples are: "I must be perfect. I must please others. If something bad happens in my life, then God must be mad at me. I am responsible for others and for their feelings."

   On a second sheet, replace each lie with a statement that reflects God's truth. For example, "I must be perfect" is changed to "I cannot be perfect, but through God's grace I am still valuable." In other words, express your understanding of how God values you and of God's ability to heal you.

2. Healing takes place from three sources: first from God, next from self, and then from others. It is, therefore, our first task to welcome God's value, acceptance, forgiveness, understanding, safety, security, belonging, and nurturing. The second task is to model these things in ourselves: If God values us, then we need to value ourselves. Third, we need to assert ourselves with others and be vulnerable regarding our needs. We can then accept other people's value of us as icing on the cake; it's the extra, but not the essential. Practice these three things through your journaling and your actions.

3. Take each of the seven truths discussed in this chapter and look for Scriptures that validate each. In your journal, express your feelings about each truth according to the Scripture journaling model at the end of Chapter 7.

4. In your journal, write about your experiences in life as related to these same Scriptures. This is especially helpful if your experience is different from the truth expressed in the Bible, since you can more readily see the differences between your life and God's truth.

Chapter 11
Illumination

"Send forth your light and your truth, let them guide me . . ."
Psalm 43:3a

True, complete healing rarely happens in an instant. While Christ was on earth, He healed some individuals instantly, but most of us experience healing as a process — often a journey of many steps. There are times along the way, though, when we experience instants of healing — moments that are healing in nature because of an "Aha" experience called illumination. Just as lightning destroys what it strikes, illumination destroys our old lies, beliefs, shames, and fears and delivers a charge from Christ to love God, self, and others in a new and dynamic way. As a result of this sudden spiritual awareness and insight, we experience a "spirit changing," or spiritual redirection.

Michelle had such a moment of insight as a result of her Scripture journaling when, for the first time, she recognized that God had purposely created her as woman. For weeks she had told me how angry she was for being a woman, an attitude that had been shaped by her childhood view of her own mother, whom she saw as being weak. Michelle viewed her adult self as being strong and tough, which she felt contradicted her sexual identity. But when she connected her femininity to the truth of the "goodness" of all of God's creation, Michelle could be at peace with herself. "I finally see that I'm not bad, but am actually treasured by Christ for being the way God created me to be," she told me. Her strength and power now come from accepting her sufficiency and wholeness in Christ.

". . . but now I see."
In the first verse of the hymn "Amazing Grace," we sing, "I once was lost, but now am found — was blind, but now I see." That poetic line describes the "before and after" of illumination. Before we receive the new insight from Christ, we are lost and blind, groping in the darkness as we react out of our woundedness and the lies we have come to accept as "truth." We bump into others with the hard turtle shell of self-protection created by our spiritually damaging dispositions and traits; and with each step, the barrier that separates us from others, including God, becomes increasingly cumbersome and oppressive.

But once illumination occurs, we have a new, personal understanding of what God has been trying to reveal to us through His Scriptures and through the life of Christ. In one moment, Christ's message becomes real to us, and we can truly experience God's grace, truth, forgiveness, and love as never before. And with that illumination, we are enabled to take another step on the road to fuller healing.

Our "Sure Peg"

In a prophesy about Jesus in Zechariah 10:4, He is characterized by a word that can be translated as "Sure Peg." This has come to be understood as a firm conviction that provides a reference point to distinguish truth from lies. Once our understanding of God's word is clarified by the Holy Spirit, Christ shines the light of His convicting spiritual truth on our lives to counteract the lies, distortions, and confusion that have blinded us to our wounds and spiritually damaging attitudes. Not only are our eyes opened to see what needs to be changed, but we also have a new, or renewed, appreciation of the grace of God that will empower us to quit responding to life with our crippling self-protection.

Notice that I said illumination comes from a Holy-Spirit-enabled understanding of God's truth. In other words, we experience the illumination of God's truth by stopping to consider what God's word says. Rarely will God take a hammer to our protective shell. But when we pause long enough to be vulnerable to the healing and transforming power of Scripture, God will slip the Sure Peg into the tiny opening we have created.

We should, then, do all that is in our power to keep the pathway clear of resistance and ask God to remove whatever obstacles remain. Since it is His desire that we be set free by the truth, He is constantly at work, directing His light in our direction. Although we can resist the truth and choose not to act on it, we cannot go back to our previous state of unknowing once we have received illumination.

A seeking heart

If we really want "insight" into baseball, we would not look for information in books about badminton or basketball. We would not go to the local golf course or skating rink, nor would we listen to the advice of professional skiers or Olympic cyclists. Instead, we would read books written by baseball players and coaches, we would watch baseball videos, go to baseball games, and ask questions of those with experience in the sport. We might spend hours hitting balls in a batting cage or join a pickup game at the park. In other words, we would diligently invest our time and energy making use of appropriate resources, taking advantage of the wisdom and experience of those who know the sport.

Likewise, if we want to receive the illumination that comes from a revelation of God's truth, we must go to the appropriate sources, for spiritual awareness and insight are a direct result of seeking His truth. God's word says, "You

A Simple Song

You were there all along.
A song
Hidden amidst the dissonance within.
My sin
Drowning out the melody. Too many notes.
So many thoughts. So many questions.
What should I do? Why am I here?
Does anybody love me? Is anybody near?
So much noise and confusion.
And then — an intrusion
Of Your love and grace.
Making space.
Cutting away the notes that were wrong.
A song
Emerging from the dark place.
Your grace
Revealing the melody pure and clear.
I can hear!
The melody of Your love
Is heard above
All the other notes, now not so many.
Harmony.
Notes that all belong
In a simple song
That one day I will raise
As a SYMPHONY of praise.

© Melody 1995

Clues to Identify Wounds

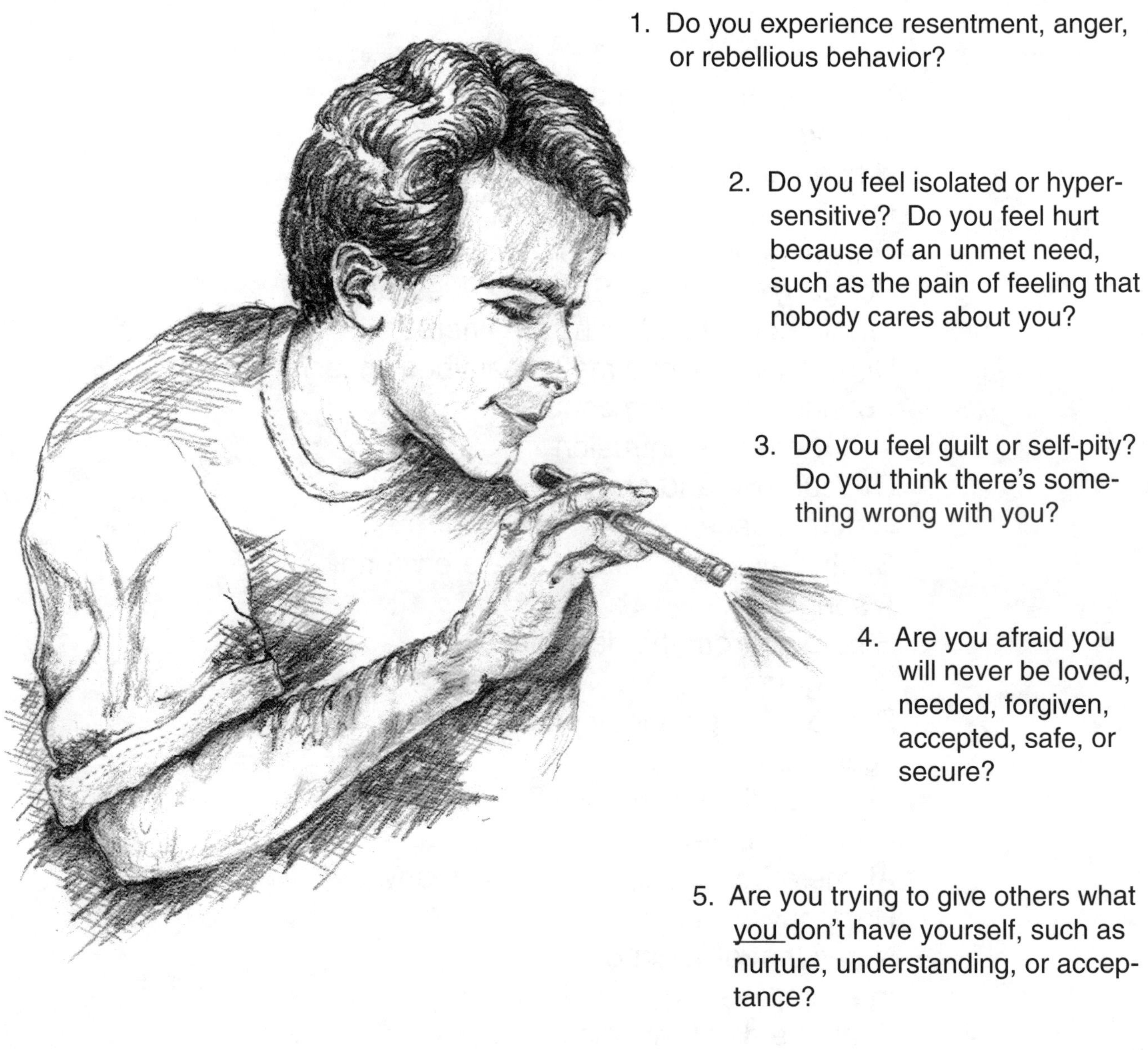

1. Do you experience resentment, anger, or rebellious behavior?

2. Do you feel isolated or hyper-sensitive? Do you feel hurt because of an unmet need, such as the pain of feeling that nobody cares about you?

3. Do you feel guilt or self-pity? Do you think there's some-thing wrong with you?

4. Are you afraid you will never be loved, needed, forgiven, accepted, safe, or secure?

5. Are you trying to give others what <u>you</u> don't have yourself, such as nurture, understanding, or accep-tance?

6. Do you deny that you have needs?

If you can answer "yes" to the questions above more than just occasionally, you know that you are suffering from wounds to your spirit.

will seek me and find me when you seek me with all your heart." (Jeremiah 29:13) That's why I give assignments to all my clients for examination of Biblical truth, Scripture journaling, individual prayer, and corporate worship and fellowship with other believers.

God's word is timeless. No matter what difficulty or tragedy we face, there is a Scriptural truth that will shine a hopeful light of illumination about our personal situation. Equipped with our heightened awareness and insight, we can experience healing of our spiritual wounds and begin to shed our self-protective covering, opening an even larger pathway through which Christ can come to us. Greater illumination can thus flow into us as the path of resistance is cleared, resulting in a charge that empowers fundamental change in the way we live.

Walk in the light

A terrific passage in Scripture talks about living in the light of illumination. "God is light; in him there is no darkness at all. If we claim to have fellowship with him yet walk in the darkness, we lie and do not live by the truth. But if we walk in the light, as he is in the light, we have fellowship with one another, and the blood of Jesus, his Son, purifies us from all sin." (I John 1:5b-7)

Once we receive illumination and see the bondage that has choked our spirit, we can choose to be freed by putting ourselves under the control of the Holy Spirit instead of just reacting out of ignorance. For once Christ has shined His light into our lives, we can never again try to justify or excuse our sins. Instead, we have new eyes to see God at work in our lives, in people, in situations, in prayer, and in worship.

When we respond in repentance, our spirits will begin an ongoing process of transformation as Christ moves within our lives. Under the guidance of the Holy Spirit, our reactions become more Christ-like. Even more importantly, we will react naturally and easily to the standard of God's love and grace, rather than trying to make it happen by the strength of our will power. We cannot "will" love or grace. They are the result of Christ's living within us and controlling our spirit.

This is our call, then, to walk in the light. And since our light comes from God's truth, it is a call to saturate ourselves in the truths of God's word by daily Bible reading and meditation on what we read there. The Holy Spirit delights in helping us understand the Scriptures. All we have to do is ask for His help in prayer before we begin reading.

1. Pray for illumination regarding your wounds or your lack of understanding about God's love, grace, or will. Illumination comes through the path of least resistance. Therefore, your prayer should ask for an openness and willingness to let God work in your life.

2. Pray: "Renew a right spirit within me." Pray this many times a day as a sentence prayer that keeps you open to the movement of healing by the Holy Spirit.

Chapter 12
Grief

"I will turn their mourning into gladness; I will give them comfort and joy instead of sorrow." Jeremiah 31:13b

Grief is the anguish or discomfort that grows out of a threat to our security with God, self, or others. Although we tend to think most often of grief as a response to the loss of a loved one through death, grief may also spring from something as ordinary as the breaking of a relationship, the loss of a job, or the disappointment we experience when our expectations are not met. All of us experience grief when our spiritual needs are not met or we encounter a threat of their not being met.

When faced with a loss, we have three choices:

1. *The pathway of denial*
The first option is the pathway of denial in which we refuse to acknowledge our hurt, grief, or loss. We avoid the pain by minimizing the wound and telling ourselves, "It wasn't that bad. I'm not that upset. I can get through this. It's in the past. What's the point?" When we minimize the significance of the event in this way, we deny the feelings we really have. When we deny our feelings of pain, we deny the underlying unmet needs. In essence, we are saying to ourselves, "I don't matter." We may avoid the hurt, but we also miss the healing that is available. When we "stuff" our feelings, the wound created by our loss also becomes infected with spiritually damaging dispositions and traits, which lead to further wounding.

We turn to performance, perfection, and achievement as a means of reestablishing our security. Hiding behind a mask, we are driven with thoughts of "I've got to - I must - I should" in order to achieve control of our situation. Or we may turn to an addiction as a way of coping — eating, drinking, working, performing, shopping, or spending rather than dealing with our pain in the God-given process of grieving.

Denying our feelings may also cause us to overreact to situations, such as bursting into tears or becoming very angry and aggressive when our plans must be canceled or when we see that we are losing control of a situation. Although we may be surprised and puzzled by our reaction, we fail to recognize that below the surface is our unresolved grief.

All of us experience grief when our spiritual needs are not met or we encounter a threat of their not being met.

Physical pain normally associated with stress, such as chronic headaches, stomach aches, and muscle tightness, may be another indicator of underlying grief, as are feelings of depression, fear, and resentment. In fact, more than 90 percent of emotional problems for which people seek professional help are related to unresolved grief. The old adage makes sense: "Pay me now, or pay me later." We will have to do the grief work sooner or later.

In one of our sessions Frank, a minister, told me about his childhood and disclosed that the two most important men in his life — his father and his grandfather — died on consecutive days. The morning after his father's death, Frank's grandfather had taken him out on the front porch to comfort him while funeral preparations were going on inside. While they were talking, his grandfather had a heart attack and died there on the porch. That same afternoon, a well-meaning aunt told 10-year-old Frank, "Now you have to be the man of the house."

The eldest of three children, Frank took that responsibility seriously, shutting down his feelings and trying to become the strong man he was expected to be. Only when he confronted his denial, control, and fear and allowed his long-buried grief to surface was he able to get in touch with all his feelings. As a result, Frank became more sensitive to his wife's needs as well as those of his parishioners.

2. Pathway of resentment

The second choice is the path of resentment, in which we feel cheated by life. Flying the banner of self-pity, we blame other people, circumstances, and ourselves rather than deal with the underlying issues. We mistakenly feel that holding on to our resentment is justified and is, therefore, our only option. We not only express our feelings, but we allow them to dominate our life. Convinced that we have been dealt a "bad hand," we ask the question "Why me?" for which there is no answer except shame and blame. As a result, we never get past the loss and remain helpless and hopeless. We don't take risks because we don't believe that anything can change. Most significantly, we can't conceive of the possibility that God's healing power can bring us comfort and peace.

3. Pathway of grief

The third choice is the pathway of grief, in which we stand on the hope (if not the conviction) that failure and loss are not the end of the story — that God can bring healing through His grace and compassion. We acknowledge our feelings and allow Christ to walk us through the natural grieving process to a place of healing and restoration. Once we allow ourselves to recognize what we are feeling (such as hurt), we can identify our need (in this case, comfort). When we know what we need, we can seek satisfaction for that need through God and others. Only then can the pain be relieved and healing take place.

This is not a question of "positive thinking," which says, "I've decided not to feel hurt." That form of mental gymnastics may deflect our attention from our pain, but since it doesn't deal with our loss, we don't really get better. Spiritual healing of grief fully acknowledges the hurt, but treats it as a symptom while at the same time focusing on the underlying cause. For in order to experience closure with our grief, we need to recognize and understand the event; forgive ourselves, others, and the situation; and commit ourselves to move beyond the loss.

The 23rd Psalm provides comfort and instruction through words that tell us we "walk through the valley of the shadow of death," with Christ as our companion. It does not say we fly over in a helicopter; neither do we "camp out" in our grief. We walk through it . . . but not alone. Grief is a journey with Christ at our side. It begins, however, with a decision to grieve.

Grief is a journey with Christ at our side.

Acknowledging the loss

The first step in the pathway of grief is to acknowledge the loss. This does not come easily in a society that values self-reliance and stoicism and where people don't know how to grieve. In many ways, grieving has become a dysfunctional cultural issue. As we were growing up, we took our cues on how to respond to death by watching our parents and other adults. If we saw them facing the loss with a controlled exterior or only token acknowledgment, we learned to feel ashamed of our grief and shut down our feelings accordingly. As a result, we don't know how to grieve, and it makes us uncomfortable to see others grieve. In fact, we unknowingly "reward" people whom we see as being "strong" in the face of loss by telling them how proud we are that they are doing "so well." Some Europeans, on the other hand, wear a black arm band for a year as a way of saying, in effect, "I'm grieving. Please show me some T.L.C."

In the face of any loss or frustration, many of us were taught, by word or example, "Don't cry. Be strong. Don't feel. Count your blessings. Get busy. Get over it. Deal with your loss alone." While some may contain a partial truth, these messages minimize our hurt or loss, and make us feel guilty for having normal feelings.

Quickly buying a new puppy the week after the family dog dies, for example, prevents children from learning to grieve properly. Telling our daughter whose heart is broken because her boyfriend broke their date to the dance, "There are other fish in the sea," trivializes her pain over being rejected. In both instances, we are teaching our children to replace what was lost instead of allowing them to learn that grief is a valid response to loss and disappointment. We give out other crippling messages to those who are grieving when we say, "Time will take care of it, time heals all wounds, or this, too, shall pass." The truth is that only if we do the grief work will time take care of the pain.

Only if we do the grief work will time take care of the pain.

Perhaps the most harmful response to someone who is grieving is the suggestion that the loss was God's will. (e.g., " God needed another little angel," or "We shouldn't question God's will in the face of death.") Instead of giving comfort, these words only prompt us to get mad at God, which separates us from the One who can truly provide comfort.

We also cause further harm when we try to stifle tears. Instead, cry and let others cry, for there is a cleansing aspect of our tears that promotes our healing. When we become stoic in the face of our pain and loss, tell our son that big boys don't cry, or otherwise urge someone who is hurting to short-circuit this natural response to physical and emotional pain, we deprive ourselves and them of a God-given, physical expression of suffering.

Stages of grief

Grief is a process, a series of stages through which we pass from woundedness and brokenness into full healing. Knowing we would experience hurt in this life, God gave us the grieving process as a means of finding our way along the path from darkness into light and life. The grief process can be broken down into stages including: shock/denial; "the blues"/sadness; isolation; anger; fear; verbalization; and acceptance.

1. **Shock/Denial** - Following a loss, many people respond first with shock and denial — not the self-imposed refusal to feel or the hiding of feelings as previously described, but an involuntary numbness that denies the loss happened. Basically, it's a physical, mental, and emotional reaction to a loss that is simply incomprehensible. Since the mind can't deal with the pain, it blocks or denies the reality of the loss. Confrontation with the loss is thus postponed until it can be absorbed. When you experience this, it's as though an anesthesia numbs the senses and cushions the mind from pain.

2. **The "Blues"/Sadness** - When the numbness wears off and reality sets in, we may enter a period of sadness. Depending on the nature of the loss or the time since the loss, the degree of discomfort may range from overwhelming, dysfunctional pain to a simple case of "the blues."

3. **Isolation** - In our grief, we may also withdraw and isolate ourselves from others, feeling that no one could possibly understand what we are experiencing.

4. **Anger** - The anger stage of grief focuses on our need to affix blame for our loss. Our resentment or outrage may be directed at ourselves, the person or situation involved in the loss, and/or God. If we "camp out" in this stage of our grieving, we enter the pathway of resentment, in which, as discussed previously, we allow our anger over the loss to dominate our life. But when it occurs as a stage of grief and not a prolonged resentment, anger is a God-given step in the process of healing from our loss.

5. **Fear** - The fear stage of the grieving process is characterized by the expectation of further loss — the proverbial "waiting for the

Let Christ hold you!

Jesus grieves when we are wounded. If you are hurting, afraid, or feeling alone — whatever your discomfort — imagine yourself crawling up into Christ's lap and letting Him hold you. No one loves and understands you quite like He does.

other shoe to drop." We are filled with anxiety — sometimes paralyzed by it — fearing that we won't be able to find another job, that our other child will have an accident, that the malignancy will return.

6. **Verbalization** - "Stop the world, I need to talk about it," expresses the sentiment of the intensely verbal stage of grieving. We need to talk about our loss. We don't want to forget any detail of it and feel driven to discuss it with others.

7. **Acceptance** - In time, we enter the stage of acceptance. Our acknowledgment of the loss and acceptance of its consequences in no way diminishes the value or importance of what we lost. But it does allow us to go on living with the comfort of Christ as our Companion and the One who meets our needs.

8. **Forgiveness** - This is an essential part of the grieving process for, along with acceptance, forgiveness brings closure to the experience of loss. Being able to forgive the person for dying, the accident for crippling, the company for downsizing — whatever the focus of our loss — along with forgiving God, completes the healing process. (More extensive information on forgiveness is presented in Chapter 14.)

Because they revolve around feelings, the stages of grief are not necessarily logical. They are fluid, meaning that we can pass from one stage to another to another, all in a matter of minutes. We don't pass neatly from one stage to another, and we may repeat some of the stages as well. Another possibility is that we may never pass through all the stages because of the unhealthy messages we have received regarding grief.

"Holy (or clean) grief" and "dirty grief"

We can distinguish grief as either "holy (clean) grief" or " dirty grief." "Dirty grief" is a form of control in which we try to find an "explanation" for our loss. When we take this path, we blame others and/or ourselves and end up with resentment and bitterness toward ourselves, others, and life in general. We may embrace "dirty grief" as a way of structuring our lives so that we will never experience hurt again. If we "know" what caused the loss, we will do everything in our power to prevent it from ever happening again. This reliance upon self excludes both the grace of God and the comfort of friends.

"Holy grief" begins with a recognition of the loss, a decision to grieve, and a willingness to depend on Christ and others to comfort and minister to us. It is a journey with Christ at our side through the stages of grief in whatever order or cycle we experience them and with the full confidence that growth and healing will result. When we surrender our pride and let go of our controlling drive to shapelife as we want it to be, we can allow Christ to heal us.

Reliance upon self excludes both the grace of God and the comfort of friends.

"Holy grief" begins with a willingness to depend on Christ.

When we surrender our pride and let go of our controlling drive to make life as we want it to be, we can allow Christ to heal us.

Assignment
Grief

Set aside 30 minutes to one hour per day for this exercise. Do only one step per day, and do not exceed your time limit because grief work is exhausting. After your prayer and journaling time, do something to nurture yourself — something that is comforting, encouraging, or supportive, such as listening to soothing music, calling a friend, reading inspirational material, or praying some more. The process of journaling opens the wound for cleansing; the nurturing activity helps put salve on the wound for healing. DO NOT DO ONE WITHOUT THE OTHER. Grief work is for <u>both</u> cleansing and healing.

1. Pray, asking the Holy Spirit to bring to your mind the memories from your past or present that need God's healing touch. Remember that, although these memories may be painful, His desire is to heal you, not to torment you. Write in your journal about what you remember.

2. Pray, asking the Holy Spirit to reveal to you what you were feeling at the time of this memory. Write in your journal about your <u>feelings</u>. For example, "I felt afraid, sad, lonely, embarrassed, violated, depressed, resentful, lost, abandoned, etc." Pray again, telling God about those feelings and asking Him to comfort you.

3. Pray, asking the Holy Spirit to reveal to you what you were <u>needing</u> at that particular time. That is, which of your spiritual needs were not fulfilled: safety, security, value, acceptance, nurturing, understanding, forgiveness (of self, others, and/or the situation), and belonging. Write in your journal about those <u>needs</u>. For example, "I needed protection and a sense of safety and security," or "I needed comforting and reassurance (nurturing and understanding)." Then go to God in prayer, asking Him to provide what you were needing. While you can't change what happened in the past, you can let go of it and get closure regarding your grief by letting Christ fill that need for you now.

4. Write a letter of compassion to yourself expressing understanding, encouragement, and comfort. For example, express to yourself "I am sorry these things have happened," followed by encouragement that things will get better. You can also send yourself a card such as is found in the categories of "Thinking of You," "You're Special," or "Friendship."

5. Distinguish your grief issues from your shame issues, i.e., holy grief from dirty grief. Write down your shame issues and destroy the list. Write down your grief issues and process them.

Chapter 13
Grace

*"From the fullness of his grace we have received
one blessing after another."* John 1:16

The grief process cleanses our wounds, but it is God's blessings that restore what was lost. While we often ask God for blessings, what we are really praying about is our "wants." Fortunately, Christ responds by providing for our spiritual needs, and the greatest blessing of all is His grace. This unmerited, loving favor from God meets and nourishes all our spiritual needs.

The parable of the Prodigal Son (Luke 15:11-32) reveals God's desire to have us feast at His banquet table of blessings. When the young man left home to seek his own way, he discovered that he couldn't make it by himself; he could not even feed himself. He was both physically hungry and spiritually empty.

Discouraged and hungry for the filling of our spiritual needs, we, too, are empty, yet we look inside ourselves or to any other source but Christ to satisfy us. But through the grieving process, we can begin to recognize our emptiness and, like the prodigal son, return to our Father for the provision of all our needs. God sets before us a banquet table of blessings in grace that will restore our joy.

We do not deserve the banquet any more than the prodigal son deserved the feast his father prepared. And since we cannot earn God's grace, it's not a matter of working our way to God's banquet table. For grace is, first and foremost, a gift from God. In order to receive the gift, we must simply admit our need for healing and grace.

Fairness or grace
We want life to be fair — or do we? Grace is beyond fair. Our concept of fair means we get what we think we deserve, while grace means that we get either less (of the punishment) or more (of the blessings) than we deserve. The choice is simple: to live either by grace or by fairness. We cannot have it both ways.

Jesus explains this concept in His parable of the workers found in Matthew 20:1-16. Some of the laborers began work early in the morning and worked

It is God's blessings that restore what was lost.

The greatest blessing of all is His grace.

Grace is beyond fair.

throughout the heat of the day. Others began only an hour before the end of the day, yet all the workers were paid the same. Is that fair? No. Is this grace? Yes, for this story is about the generosity of the Master. Grace is an expression of Christ's generosity towards us. Therefore, we must leave our "fair" thinking behind and move toward receiving the blessings of grace. Grace is beyond fair — for this we can be thankful.

Many people regard the presentation of God in the Old Testament as describing a harsh God of vengeance and judgment, while in reality it is a testimony of His grace. The children of Israel, called to be God's own people, continually forfeited God's blessing and protection by disobeying His law and following the practices of the idolatrous people around them. Again and again, God forgave their stubborn self-will and rescued, restored, and blessed them. His provision of grace to the Israelites is extended to us as well. Rather than withdraw from us when we turn our back and walk away from Him, God continues to initiate relationship with us.

Necessity of grace
Grace without judgment is an empty concept, for grace is made necessary by the fact that we are judged by God for the way we live our lives. While He calls us to be increasingly Christ-like, we will not achieve that high standard this side of heaven. Until that time, God has to provide a way to fill the gap between our behavior and the standard of perfection established by Christ. That's grace, and we receive it through humble confession and repentance.

Our problem is that, instead of repenting, we say that the standard is unfair and God is judgmental, and blame God for our inability to measure up. Or, like the prodigal son's older brother who thought he could earn his father's favor through his actions, we ignore the fact of our sinfulness and try to be perfect in our own strength, becoming performance-oriented. Then we feel guilty and full of shame when we fail and still wonder why we are not experiencing God's grace.

Worse yet, we may lower Christ's standard by making excuses for, or rationalizing, our behavior in such a way that we think we don't need grace. This results in situational ethics: "It was O.K.; no big deal." When we lower the standard God sets before us, we cheapen grace and ignore the fact that it cost God the life of His only Son. The bottom line is: The only way to keep the standard is to accept what God offers us to make up for the discrepancy.

Grace meets needs of our spirit
In addition to closing the gap, grace meets every one of the eight needs of our spirit:
1. Grace provides safety — the ability to truly be ourselves, knowing that God will not abandon us.
2. Grace provides security through the safekeeping of God's guidance, direction, and strength.
3. Grace provides value by giving meaning, purpose, significance, and worth to our lives without our having to achieve an

Rather than withdraw from us when we turn our back and walk away from Him, God continues to initiate relationship with us.

When we lower the standard God sets before us, we cheapen grace and ignore the fact that it cost God the life of His only Son.

impossible standard.

4. Grace indicates acceptance of ourselves as God created us.
5. Grace encompasses nurturing by providing comfort, encouragement, and loving care.
6. Grace includes understanding because nowhere are we more understood than in the presence of the grace of God who created us.
7. Grace brings forgiveness and redemption.
8. Grace involves a sense of belonging because intimacy and connection occur when we are surrounded by the grace of God.

Grace brings healing.

Steve was a young man whose wife had left him because of what she called coldness and indifference. While growing up, his father's very stern, perfectionistic manner left no room for mistakes. Failure to comply with the rigid rules resulted in being shunned by his father, as though he wasn't part of the family. Understandably, this conditional acceptance left Steve unable to comprehend unconditional love from his Heavenly Father or accept love even from his wife.

Once Steve identified his wounds and the ways he had sought to hide his pain and protect himself, he sought healing in God's love by accepting it in faith, even thought he didn't yet feel it. When he allowed God to give him a sense of value and acceptance, Steve's life changed as he became more sensitive to others and more open and honest in relationships.

Do you want to be healed?

In John 5:1-8 there is the story of a crippled man who lay by the pool of Bethesda. Legend said that whoever got into the pool first when the waters moved would be healed. This particular man had been an invalid for 38 years. In all that time, someone always got into the water ahead of him. One day Jesus walked by and saw the man lying near the pool. He asked the man, "Do you want to be healed?" The crippled man replied, in effect, "Yes, but you don't understand . . . " He then outlined all of the ways he had tried to bring about his own healing and why he had failed.

Does this sound familiar? We, too, have a list of reasons why healing hasn't occurred in our lives. We are too bad; we haven't worked hard enough; our lives are too chaotic. The list is endless, for we are focusing on our efforts and fail to seek God's grace. Remember, Jesus asked, "Do you want to be healed?" This is a haunting question. Are we willing to give up our self-reliance and depend instead on God's unconditional and unmerited grace? His grace defies rational thought. It is a gift beyond our comprehension.

The question remains, "Do you want to be healed?" Christ stands ready with His grace to heal us and meet all of our spiritual needs. Say "yes" to the healing that is available through God's grace.

We have a list of reasons why healing hasn't occurred in our lives . . . for we are focusing on our efforts and fail to seek God's grace.

The Journey of Life Game

The Journey of Life Game consists of two parts: the Grace Game and the Satan Game. Your day-to-day life is filled with circumstances that require you to make choices, some of which are very simple. Others, however, are much more difficult, and are often veiled in uncertainties. Much the same as in a child's board game where moves are determined by a roll of the dice, each move in the Journey of Life Game varies according to the choices you make as your life unfolds.

You are allowed to select a Grace Card, if you choose. There are five such cards, and although each records a different promise, all five say virtually the same thing — that God is <u>always</u> there to comfort, strengthen, and guide you. These cards don't guarantee you a worry-free life, but they do assure you that you don't have to "go it alone." God's Grace Cards are free and can be used at any stage of the game.

The toughest part of the game is now before you. Although many of your decisions carry no hidden penalty, there are also choices that result in your being given a Satan Card as well. These aren't always easy to spot, for the top side is generally very appealing, whereas the flip side reveals one of Satan's lies. Temptations and promises; lies, fear, and shame . . . Why would anyone choose a Satan Card? You've done so many times. He strikes where you are most vulnerable. Let's look at some examples.

Your volunteer time, spent helping others less fortunate, is vital to your community. But should you draw a Satan Card, he is quick to demean and criticize your ability should you make even the slightest mistake. An opportunity to invite a new neighbor to church, should you draw a Satan Card, can fill you with fears of rejection and uncertainty. He loves to take your daily life and twist the circumstances to cause you self-doubt and feelings of loneliness or being unloved.

Satan has built a jail for you. The walls are made from your own woundedness and your spiritually damaging dispositions and traits. This jail entraps you and causes you to "lose turns," while he continues aiming destructive thoughts and feelings at you. His lies so wound your spirit that it begins to grow anxious and wither. Your heart and mind become hardened to God's words of comfort and hope. In this game, Satan's jail is not just a square on the board. Once you've traded God's protection for Satan's insecurity and God's blessings for Satan's addictions, this jail becomes your life. You can stay in jail for as long as you like, trying to solve all of your problems yourself or trying to control the situation. Or you can use your Grace Card to get out of jail!

Once you've been freed, the game rules require that you write down what you've learned from this experience as well as the promise of God that you've seen verified, such as, "I don't have to worry, because God has promised to meet all my needs according to His glorious riches in Christ Jesus," or "I am never alone, for God is with me." Keep the record of your lesson as a reminder for the next time Satan tries to fool you with his lies and accusations. You never play the Journey of Life Game without a supply of God's Grace Cards available for use at any time!

Assignment
Grace

1. Do the following imagery exercise: Close your eyes and imagine that you are lying across your bed crying. Something upsetting has happened in your life. You are thinking a variety of thoughts, such as, "What's wrong with me? Why did I do it this way? Why didn't I do it differently? I'm never going to get any better. Rejected again. I deserved it." These messages are expressions of shame. Another part of you says, "But next time I will . . . " The list is endless about how it could be different. These are expressions of control.

Imagine now that Jesus walks into this scene. He comes into your room and sits beside you. He is carrying a large gift. He calls you by name and says, "I have a gift for you. I want to give you this gift. You didn't earn it, and you didn't do anything to deserve it. I simply want to give it to you, but you cannot receive this gift as long as your hands are clenched holding on to other things. You have to let go of them before you can receive this gift. It is the gift of worth in God's eyes."

Curious, you now sit up on thebed. You look down, and sure enough, your hands are clenched so tightly that your knuckles are white. Jesus speaks again and says, "In your right hand is shame. Shame is the attitude that convinces you that you're a failure; you're worthless; you're unloved. But I have to be honest with you: this is also your security. Your shame allows your life to remain predictable and familiar. Life may be painful, but at least it's secure. So in order to receive my gift to you, you're going to have to let go of the shame. Will you let go of it?"

If you answer "yes," Jesus takes the shame and throws it out the window, then closes and locks the window, saying, "I don't need shame; you don't need shame. It's gone." He then continues, "In your left hand is control. This attitude convinces you that there is a right way to think, act, feel, and believe. If you can just figure it out, everything will be wonderful in your life. This is your hope, though it is false. In order to receive my gift, you have to give up control. Will you let go of it?"

If you answer "yes," Christ takes the control, places it in His pocket, saying "I am the one who will be in control of your life now." He then hands the gift to you. It is wrapped, and you open it with anticipation. Inside is the most beautiful white coat you have ever seen. Christ helps you put it on as He explains its meaning. "It is white for purity because you have been completely cleansed and forgiven. It is a coat for protection and comfort against the difficulties in life. You will be faced with hurts, but this coat will help you get through them Look inside and you will see that it is lined — lined with truth that you are my child. Nothing can penetrate this lining or destroy this truth.

"Look inside your right pocket. Remember? You thought when you gave up shame that you gave up security. See, I have placed in your pocket true security that comes from grace. Nothing you can do can stop me from loving you. Now look in your left pocket. Remember? When you gave up control, you thought you gave up hope. I have placed inside your left pocket true hope that comes from being wholly yourself and being responsible for yourself rather than trying to please others.

"Your collar is the peace that will surround you as my child. You also have the sash of joy that will encompass you as well. Remember that this is a gift, and I will never take it back. You did not earn this; I gave it to you because I love you."

Soak in the feelings that this imagery brings and experience Christ's gift of grace.

2. Read Hebrews 10:22, 23. Write in your journal what this Scripture says about the completeness of God's grace apart from our works.

3. Pray the following prayer for a minimum of seven days: "Give me the eyes of Christ to see myself as Christ sees me."

At the end of the seven days, write a letter of blessing from Christ to you. A blessing is about unconditional love, approval, appreciation, and acceptance in all these areas: your physical characteristics, your personality characteristics, your talents and abilities, and your spiritual gifts. Remember this is a letter from God who created you and loves you completely. This can be the most healing experience for you, but remember you will only get a minuscule idea of the true depth of God's love. He loves us beyond our comprehension, but even a portion of understanding will transform your life. Read your blessing letter a minimum of five times a day so that it becomes a "soaking" meditation.

4. Make a list of needs, feeling, and beliefs. Take these to Christ in prayer for grace to meet, comfort, and transform.

5. You may also ask Christ to write you a letter of blessing (see No.3 above) regarding a specific unmet need.

6. Spend 15 minutes each day in play. Play is an activity that has no purpose and involves no competition, where you spend time enjoying the creation of life itself. These activities can be walking, observing butterflies, swinging at the park -- anything you consider play. Play can be a very spiritual activity because in it you are being yourself, and you are allowing God to be present.

Chapter 14
Forgiveness

"Bear with each other and forgive whatever grievances
you may have against one another. Forgive
as the Lord forgave you." Colossians 3:13

Forgiveness is essential for our healing, for it cleanses us of hurt, anger, and resentment. It is the passageway from self-protection to vulnerability, taking us toward the abundant life that Jesus described. Unforgiveness, on the other hand, limits our future because it prevents us, and others, from making the changes that will help us grow past the hurt. Sometimes we feel justified in not forgiving and hold on to our grudges with determination. Yet there can also be times when we fail to recognize the need for forgiveness because we see the other person's behavior or abuse as "normal" or somehow warranted.

In a seeming paradox, unforgiveness is damaging whether we are unforgiving as a deliberate choice or out of our ignorance of the need to forgive. For even when we don't recognize the need to forgive, we may continue to believe the lies that grew out of our hurt, regardless of how we've glossed over the circumstances.

In reality, we have all failed in our Christian walk. We must, therefore, forgive ourselves and others for not being perfect. If we don't, we become imprisoned in our shame and blame. We must also forgive illness and accidents that hurt or take someone away from us, as well as the circumstances, such as corporate "downsizing," that cause suffering in our life. In addition, we must forgive God — not because He needs our forgiveness, but because we blame God as part of our grieving. He is the "fall guy," the catchall for what we can't explain. While it may be irrational to blame Him, our feelings, nevertheless, are real. Forgiving God is something we do for our own good in order to be cleansed of the resentment that inhibits our relationship with Him.

Forgiveness is God-ordained. Scripture is full of references to the necessity of forgiveness, such as in the verses that follow what we know as the Lord's Prayer: "For if you forgive men when they sin against you, your heavenly Father will also forgive you. But if you do not forgive men their sins, your

Forgiveness is essential for our healing.

Forgiving God is something we do for our own good in order to be cleansed of the resentment that inhibits our relationship with Him.

Father will not forgive your sins." (Matthew 6:14-15) Two other references are in Mark 11:25 and Luke 6:37.

The ugly alternative

Forgiveness is a God-ordained and God-enabled choice that we make. Our other option — unforgiveness — is not an attractive alternative. In addition to not being God's will for us, unforgiveness limits our future; for when we don't forgive, we don't give ourselves and others the opportunity for change and growth. Even when we withhold forgiveness in some particular situation because we're not aware of the need to forgive, we unconsciously limit our ability to be healed. Purposely withholding forgiveness can have even uglier consequences.

Unforgiveness is like drinking poison and expecting someone else to die. That sounds like an overly harsh statement, but when we feel justified in not forgiving and attempt to protect ourselves by controlling circumstances (to punish the other person or at least keep them at a distance), the only result is further harm to us instead. Not only do we continue operating with the spiritually damaging disposition of unforgiveness, we become further crippled by judgmentalism and a critical spirit. The good news is that Christ is willing to come along side us in our suffering and offer us the antidote of forgiving through Him.

Recognizes the hurt

Rather than denying our pain, forgiveness begins with recognition of the fact that we have been hurt. By holding the person, situation, God, and/or ourselves responsible for behavior, we say, in effect, "It happened." Most of us, instead, make excuses or rationalize behavior through such statements as: "But they didn't mean to. They didn't know what they were doing. They were doing the best they could." Although these statements may be correct, they take the focus away from our hurt. We cannot begin to heal if we deny our own hurt. God gives us the process of forgiveness as the oil of healing because He knows that we will be hurt in this life.

Our need to admit the existence of our hurt does not mean that we have the right to judge someone else's intent, motivation, or purpose, although we do have the right to judge their behavior. It's appropriate to say, "He did this," but we should not say, "He did this and, therefore, he is a bad person. He meant to do it; he wanted to hurt me." These statements would indicate we are judging the individual's heart, which only God can do.

Not a matter of forgetting

It is important to understand that forgiving does not mean forgetting. If you have physical scars, you certainly remember the event that caused them. We have spiritual and emotional scars as well, but we often think of these scars only in a negative sense. Although a scar from a physical wound may be unattractive, it is proof of the wound's healing. So too can the scar from a spiritual or emotional wound give proof of God's healing. Otherwise we would still be "bleeding" from these wounds.

Years ago, the daughter of my friend Kay was injured in a fall over the side of her sandbox. A splinter from the weathered wood punctured the flesh on Adrienne's leg beside her shin bone. Kay pulled out the wood fragment and put antibiotic ointment and a bandage on the wound. In time, a scab developed, although the area remained sensitive to touch. Several weeks later while helping the toddler wash her hair in the bathtub, Kay noticed the scab had softened and partially fallen off. When she held Adrienne's leg to examine the wound, the child cried out as pus and a sliver of brown wood emerged from deep in her leg. More than 20 years later, the small scar on Adrienne's leg is a reminder of the childhood injury as well as the healing that took place after the "bad stuff" was fully cleansed from the wound.

Forgiveness is a cleansing process that enables us to release the "bad stuff" from deep within and helps a scar to form over what would otherwise be a painful, festering wound. The difference is that while we haven't forgotten what we have forgiven, the memory no longer has power to hurt us. When Christ returned to earth after His resurrection, He showed His disciples the scars on His hands and side. Those scars were not removed; they were simply transformed by the resurrection. Likewise, our spiritual and emotional scars are not removed or forgotten, but are transformed by God's grace into experiences we can use to help others find healing for their hurts.

While we haven't forgotten what we have forgiven, the memory no longer has power to hurt us.

Not reconciliation

Forgiveness and reconciliation are two different issues. Forgiveness is singular: a responsibility that is totally independent of the other person's knowledge, willingness, agreement, or cooperation. In fact, we are called to forgive others, even if they are no longer alive. We are not blocked from healing because the other person does not recognize our wound, nor are we required to resume our relationship with the person or situation that created the wound. It's a matter of making the decision to forgive because Christ requires it.

We are called to forgive others, even if they are no longer alive.

Reconciliation, on the other hand, is a choice made by individuals to meet "halfway" under the lordship of Christ to reestablish a relationship. It requires that both (or all) parties recognize the wound and the need for change, and that they agree on the terms and conditions necessary to restore the relationship. This is the principle under which guidelines or understandings are determined by mutual agreement in order for husbands and wives to rebuild their marriage.

To help you understand the difference between forgiveness and reconciliation, let's use an example of financial debt. If a person borrows $100 and doesn't repay the loan, forgiveness cancels the debt. However if the person comes back wanting to borrow another $100, then reconciliation would require conditions. The first $100 is in the past, and we close the door to the past through forgiveness. Reconciliation sets up guidelines for the borrowing of the second $100, such as a structured payment plan or the giving of collateral. Notice that reconciliation requires forgiveness as the first step.

Taking back our power

If someone tells us repeatedly that we are stupid and will never amount to anything, we can choose how we will respond. One approach is to comply by agreeing with the statement and never trying to accomplish anything. Or we may say, in rebellion, "I'll show him. I'll get my Ph.D." In either of these responses, we are controlled by that person. We have allowed their words and opinions about us to determine our behavior.

The path of forgiveness, on the other hand, breaks that control by saying, "I will forgive you for what you said and will, instead, listen to God's truth about me." Then we are free to become what God would have us be, rather than being tied by either compliance or rebellion.

Bondage of unforgiveness

There is an essential truth about unforgiveness: We become what we do not forgive. Debbie first came to my office when she brought her daughter, Emily, to me for counseling because their strained relationship had become hostile. In our initial meeting it became clear that Debbie had a very strict, critical, and demanding attitude toward Emily. In a separate session with her, I asked Debbie to describe the relationship she had with her own mother. She told me about a very tense childhood and youth under the watchful eye of a stern and domineering woman whom she could never please. "No matter what I did, it was never right or enough," she told me through a flood of angry tears. "At first, I turned myself inside out trying to please Mother, but it was impossible."

Feeling justified in her anger toward her mother, Debbie bristled at my suggestion that it was time to forgive her. Only when she recognized that she was repeating this destructive pattern of parenting with her own daughter was she motivated to forgive her mother. Not only did her relationship with Emily improve, but she became less demanding and critical, as well as more accepting and loving, in other relationships as well.

Debbie was, in effect, in bondage to the spirit of her mother whom she had not forgiven. As she so accurately put it: " I'm just like Mother." This bondage to the one we haven't forgiven is seen most clearly in cycles of abuse. If we have been abused, we will abuse — maybe not in the same way someone abused us, but we will still abuse others. If we have been manipulated, we will manipulate. Forgiveness breaks the bondage of our spirit to the other person's spirit and allows us to be joined to the Holy Spirit.

The Bridge to the Divine

Forgiveness is the bridge that, more than anything else, connects us to the Divine. It requires Christ working through us to release us from the bondage of self-protection. Forgiveness reignites our passion for the Savior. Does your life reflect Christ's presence?

A divine work

We are not capable of forgiveness apart from Jesus Christ. Left to the attitude of our fallen human nature, we want to get even and to hurt those who cause us pain. At the very least, we want them to understand how much they have hurt us. The necessity in healing, then, is for us to be willing to let go of the weight of unforgiveness so that God can lift it from us. Keep in mind that forgiveness is for our healing, not for the other person.

Forgiveness is divine — a work of God. We make a decision to forgive, but it is God's Spirit in us who does the forgiveness work. Christ on the cross is our example and model. He said, " Father, (you) forgive them . . . " (Luke 23:34) He didn't say, "I forgive them." We make a decision of the will to forgive, but then we ask God to forgive through us. Christ completes the process by cleansing our spirits of resentments, fears, shame, hurt, or anything else that blocks the channel of forgiveness. Our wound is thus transformed through God's grace.

Cleansing our spiritual vessel

The primary focus of spiritual, or inner, healing is increasing our capacity to love, which requires that we examine what is blocking our understanding or the flow of God's love through our spirit. A wonderful Scripture is found in Romans 5:5, which says that God pours His love into our hearts by the Holy Spirit. Love is not a personality characteristic but a spiritual quality — one of the fruits of the Spirit. In order for us to be loving, we need to be an open vessel through which God's love can flow freely. If we have not been able to "get over" some wound or hurt, unforgiveness keeps the vessel of our spirit encrusted with bitterness, hurt, fear, and shame. Forgiveness is like a Roto-Rooter® drain cleaner that breaks the crust to release the hurt and keeps our spirit vessel open and available to God, thus enabling us to become the person God wants us to be. As our feelings are released, we may experience pain, but the end result will be a healthier spirit.

Many people believe the misconception that forgiveness brings a feeling of elation. It does not. If there is a feeling associated with forgiveness, it is that of letting go — of release. For when we forgive, we yield up the heavy burden of our pain and our spiritually damaging dispositions and traits. Forgiveness may also put us in touch, for the first time, with suppressed feelings of loss, sadness, or pain. But through the process of forgiveness, we can release these feelings to Christ. As a result our spirit will become softer and more pleasing to God.

Bridge to the divine

Finally, then, forgiveness is the bridge that more than anything else connects us with the divine, for it requires Christ's working through us to release us from the bondage of our self-protection. Forgiveness rescues us from the attitudes of our destructive dispositions, allowing for the production of the fruits of the spirit. Left in place, the crust of self-protection mars the image of Christ within us, whereas forgiveness allows Christ's image in us to come alive again.

Assignment
Forgiveness

Note: There is greater explanation and an example of this assignment on the following pages.

1. Make a list of <u>things</u>, <u>persons</u>, <u>events</u>, and <u>behaviors</u> you need to forgive. Your hurts, angers, and fears may be indicators to help you identify the event(s) or the behaviors of others that have caused your pain. (e.g., physical/sexual abuse, perfectionist parent, early death of parent, etc.)

2. Identify how your spirit is in bondage to a person or situation that you have not forgiven.

3. Identify your <u>feelings</u> with regard to each event or behavior. (e.g., fear, depression, anger, sadness, etc.)

4. Identify the <u>beliefs</u> you have about yourself as a result of the event or behavior. (e.g., I'm not good enough; I don't matter; I must be perfect; etc.)

5. Ask Christ to cleanse you of <u>one</u> issue and its beliefs and feelings per day by praying:

"Lord, please forgive _(person)_ for _(event/behavior)_. It made me feel _(feelings)_ and I believed _(beliefs)_. I ask You to forgive _(person)_ for not perfectly loving me. Please forgive me for believing the lie and not believing You. Lord, comfort my feelings. Please let your forgiveness for _(person)_ flow through me. Let me be a vessel for Your forgiveness. Amen."

6. Put the date of your prayer of forgiveness beside the person/event/behavior in No.1 above as you apply God's healing grace to that hurt.

113

The Forgiveness Work

The purpose of this assignment, which I refer to as "doing the forgiveness work," is to bring closure to an issue that you have dealt with thoroughly. Although it will result in emotional healing for you, completing the exercise is in no way connected to whether or not you receive the other person's forgiveness.

Forgiveness is about freeing yourself from the power of the lies that another's sinful behavior has led you to accept as truth. In other words, you are saying, "I choose to forgive you for the lies so that I will not carry this anger (or other emotion you feel) for another minute!" If you are so emotionally trapped that you cannot imagine yourself ever being able to forgive someone, your prayer then becomes, "God, I <u>choose</u> to forgive _____ for _____. Begin the healing work of forgiveness in me." That's all there is to it!

Focus on the forgiveness prayer throughout the day, and at day's end, write the date in your journal to indicate that it has been accomplished. You may choose to have a little ceremony with your written record of who and what you have forgiven to "celebrate" this healing accomplishment, if you like, such as burning it, flushing it down a toilet, tearing it up, or mailing it (if you feel it would be appropriate). The choice is yours — to feed the hatred, anger, loss, etc., or to feed the peace. Remember that the comfort part is crucial in this exercise.

The following is an example of one client's approach to this assignment.

Issue:

"My mother never bonded with me, before or after my birth."

How this made me feel:

"As I began to see the truth of this issue, I was deeply affected, feeling extremely abandoned. I seldom felt close to her and didn't particularly admire her nor want to emulate her. We pushed against one another throughout my teen years. I rarely felt the comfort and nurturing that I'm sure I needed. I have spent a lifetime being needy, with a skewed understanding of feminine and masculine roles."

The lie I took from this:

"I believed that I must not have been worthy of bonding with Mom, that I was an unappealing, unattractive, difficult-to-manage, and flawed child to cause a mother not to fully bond. As an adult, I believed I was unworthy of bonding with family or friends, and that only the most desperate would want to bond with me. I believed that my understanding of masculine and feminine roles was accurate and everyone else's, probably even God's, were false and unfair. I believed that I was not as good as my brother and sister, and could never be anyone's favorite — then or now. If your mother can't bond with you, who would want to?"

God's truth:

"The truth is that God will bond with anyone who asks Him, as I did years ago when I accepted Christ into my life. But I don't think I fully realized just what a bond with Him truly meant. He knew me before I was born, knew the life that was before me. I was His child. He had called me by name, and when I responded, I became His. We are bonded to one another: Him to me, and me to Him. He will nurture and comfort me, if I ask. I am worthy in His eyes, equal to my siblings — to everyone. Only He loves me 100%, in spite of my sinful nature. He can and will be all those things my mother either did not, or could not, be for me. He can and will teach me all about proper masculine and feminine roles. I'm just a little stubborn, so He's got His work cut out for Him there."

God's comfort:

"Comfort me, O Lord, when I forget about your desire to have me always feel bonded to You. Reassure me daily that I am worthy of Your love, always and forever. Let me lean on You during those times when I don't understand life and when I feel rejected, unloved, unappreciated, needy. Nurture me, Lord. Treasure me for who I am and cherish me for the woman I strive to become. Hold me close to You that I might feel the warmth and tenderness that I needed long ago, but did not receive. Bridge the gaps within me so that I might, at long last, feel whole and complete."

The forgiveness:

"Lord, I choose to forgive Mom for her lack of bonding with me, whether intentional or not. I choose to put her actions, her lies, her lack of nurture and comfort into the past, where they rightfully belong. I understand fully that my actions and behaviors, as an adult, are my responsibility, and that holding her accountable for my shortcomings is pointless. I no longer want to deal with the anger, resentment, and loss. Help me, Lord, to focus on what could have been, had our circumstances been different. Take away — forever — the sadness and emptiness that I feel at the very core of my being. I pray that You will begin the healing work of forgiveness, through me, at this very moment."

Date:

******

Chapter 15
Oppression

*"The Lord is a refuge for the oppressed, a stronghold in
times of trouble. Those who know your name will trust in you,
for you, Lord, have never forsaken those who seek you."*
Psalm 9:9-10

The dictionary defines oppression as the state of being heavily weighed down
mentally or spiritually by unjust or tyrannical use of force or authority. It
implies being subjugated, persecuted, overwhelmed or crushed in spirit or
mind. The root word, in fact, means "pressed down."

These are dark terms for a state that most Christians experience in some
degree or other during their lives. Because it keeps us from participating in
the abundant life that Christ came to bring, oppression prevents us from
becoming all that God created us to be. Christ wants to release us from the
bondage of oppression and give us freedom, but He will not do so until we
have spiritual healing.

Our spiritually damaging dispositions/traits, our addictions, and Satan himself
are the agents of oppression in our lives. Since we choose, for the most part,
how we will respond to the damaging power of the past, much of the
oppression we suffer is essentially self-inflicted. Remember that our
spiritually damaging dispositions are attitudes that we take on as a self-
protecting response to the wounds to our spirit (wounds to the mind, heart,
and body passing through to the spirit and wounds caused by starving the
spirit of its needs).

*Since we choose, for the
most part, how we will
respond to the damaging
power of the past, much
of the oppression we
suffer is essentially
self-inflicted.*

Breaking the power of the past
Ben sought my help because he was suffering from debilitating anxiety
attacks. As a result of spiritual abuse by his parents and the church he had
attended while growing up, he even questioned his salvation. Ben was trying
to live up to impossible standards, feeling that he was not worthy if he was
not perfect. Believing that he had to be saved all over again every time he
sinned, Ben was afraid he would go to hell if he failed to recognize some sin
in his life. His fear of God was crippling him.

In the light of God's truth, Ben came to a new understanding of God's grace and full acceptance of him on the basis of Christ's blood instead of Ben's efforts. He is now healed and participating in the fullness of life that was always available to him.

Another client, Ellen, struggled with attitudes of shame and control that grew out of her not feeling valued. As a result, she poured all her energy into being "good enough" so that others would appreciate her. In time she identified the cause of this wound but found it difficult to do Scripture journaling about her value as God's child. Shortly afterward, the company for which she worked was bought by another company, and all of the employees were interviewed in advance of staff reorganization. Ellen came to see me following her interview, filled with discouragement because she had not been given much praise.

Two weeks later, Ellen was not only still employed, she had been given her manager's job and a corresponding salary increase. The new company chose not to counter a competing offer her manager had received from a competitor. On his way out of the office she was about to move into, he told her, "They said they wouldn't try to keep me since they had you to do the job." My excited response was cut short as Ellen lamented, "I feel so badly. If it weren't for me, he would still have his job." I couldn't believe my ears. Ellen was so oppressed by her shame and control that, even when she was given unmistakable recognition for her value to the company, she couldn't hear it or receive it. Was it any wonder she found it difficult to grasp God's truth about her worth?

Oppressed by our "security blanket"

When we are wounded, we reach for our spiritually damaging dispositions and traits as a security blanket to protect ourselves from further pain or wounding. This blanket of self- protection becomes oppressive because it is a barrier to healing. Every time we try to prevent the hurt rather than let Christ minister to us, we are living outside the plan that God ordained for us as His children. As a result, we lose our spiritual blessings such as value, acceptance, safety, and security and are left with a withered spirit that is dried up and depleted.

Every time we try to prevent the hurt rather than let Christ minister to us, we are living outside the plan that God ordained for us as His children.

It is not God's desire for us to live oppressed lives. Christ tells us in Matthew 7:11, "If you, then, though you are evil, know how to give good gifts to your children, how much more will your Father in heaven give good gifts to those who ask him!" But God removed His hand of blessing and protection from the children of Israel when they rejected Him and followed other gods. Like them, we will miss out on all that God would give us if we turn away from Him by stubbornly clinging to our means of protection.

Oppressed by addictions

It doesn't matter whether our addiction is to food, work, perfection, alcohol, or some other chemical substance, an addiction is another form of oppressive, self-persecution. While the focus of our addiction may be to control or escape our circumstances, the end result is that we are further blinded to our spiritually damaging dispositions. Unfortunately, the " fallout" on the people close to an addict broadens the scope of oppression, for they are forced to deal with the addiction, not just the individual.

Another danger is that the obsessive/compulsive nature of addiction shifts the focus of our life away from God — in some cases, to the point of idolatry. Chemical substance abuse also serves as an open invitation for Satan to oppress and afflict us while our defenses are broken down.

An opportunistic enemy

When walking around barefooted, we don't think about the germs that thrive in our environment. As long as they remain outside the body, they are harmless. But when the protective covering of skin on our foot is sliced open, harmful bacteria invade the wound and increase our discomfort. Satan is just such an opportunistic enemy, for like the bacteria that contaminate the cut, Satan will infect the wounds to our spirit with his lies, accusations, and distortions.

If, for example, our spirit wound is a lack of feeling value, Satan twists reality and moves into our thoughts with painful barbs such as, "You're not good enough," or "You'll never amount to anything." If we don't question it, Satan's lie will become our pervasive thinking about every aspect of our life. Our problem is that 90 percent of the time we don't recognize what's happening, and we believe Satan's put-downs as being truth about us. We can choose to resist Satan by filling our heart, mind, and spirit with the Biblical truths about how God sees us.

Although Jesus openly acknowledged his existence, many Christians don't like to think, talk, or read about Satan. But the fact remains that he is as real as God is. Many of my clients are resistant at first to consider that Satan has a role in their misery. That suits Satan just fine, since his greatest weapon is our ignorance. When we don't recognize what we're dealing with, he can make our life a living hell. If we simply try to "be good," think positively, feel happy, or change our behavior, we will fail miserably, for Satan will continue to torment us. He is sneakier and more deceptive than any earthly enemy we will ever face.

Strongholds

In order to oppress us, all Satan needs is an entry point. Whether it is through the wounds to our spirit, our spiritually damaging dispositions and traits by which we respond, our addictions, or our other sins, Satan can use these as his entry point for ongoing oppression. In time he can become entrenched, creating strongholds — areas in which our thoughts, beliefs, feelings, and, ultimately, our will are under his influence, if not domination. I'm not talking about demonic possession here. Simply stated, when we sin or have been wounded by someone else's sin, we are open to harassment from Satan.

The obsessive/compulsive nature of addiction shifts the focus of our life away from God.

Satan will infect the wounds to our spirit with his lies, accusations, and distortions.

Satan's greatest weapon is our ignorance.

The Shame/Control Game

Most of us are taught the Shame/Control Game very early in life; its rules are quite simple. The game board is the world you live in, and your experiences and relationships are your stack of "Stuff" cards to draw from. You don't need a token or game piece because you won't be <u>going</u> anywhere — just back and forth, back and forth. Although you will need a special coin to flip, there are no prizes at the end — only losses. The game will last as long as you can stand to play it, and although you play it by yourself, others may end up being dragged into the game as well.

A sample round would go something like this: You draw a card from the "Stuff" pile that says, "Your teenager just said that his grade-point average wasn't high enough to allow him to go on the special field trip." Now you toss the coin, and it says, "Shame." Here's the easy part: You have to think of a reason for <u>you</u> to feel ashamed about this situation, such as, "If I weren't so dumb, my kid wouldn't be dumb either," or "If I weren't having to work to help make ends meet, I could have been at home where I belong, making sure my kids study more." (See how you've brought in other people and another reason to feel guilty!)

Now that you're feeling really rotten, you flip the coin over to "Control." Your choices may be, "I'll ask my boss if I can leave work earlier so that I can make sure the kids are studying," or "Maybe I'll take away one of his privileges so he'll learn his lesson," or "I'll go straight to the principal so that his teacher will have to let him go."

At this point in the game, you've had your "stuff" happen, you've felt rightfully ashamed, and then attempted to take control of the situation. If you follow through with any of the control solutions, you'll quickly find that control doesn't work either. You flip the coin back over to "Shame" and treat yourself to <u>another</u> round of guilt. Then flip the coin over to "Control" and, once again, try to "fix" the situation.

It's an exercise in futility: Shame/Control, Shame/Control. And although there are no prizes, you <u>do</u> get something when the game is over: You get smaller and weaker and closer to the realization that "There <u>has</u> to be a better way!"

This is one of the reasons why Bible study, meditation on the word of God, and appropriation of God's truths are essential for all believers. When our wounds and destructive attitudes are cleansed, we must fill ourselves with God's truth and grace before we can experience healing. That is to say, when we evict Satan from our strongholds, we must call on the Holy Spirit to fill these once dark places with the light of God.

The danger in leaving out the step of "refilling" with God is that Satan can otherwise move back in. As is recorded in Matthew 12:43-45, if Satan finds our "house unoccupied," he returns with seven other spirits more wicked than himself. Whether or not we take this literally, the point is that once we sweep our "house" clean and put it in order (receive cleansing for our wounds and spiritually damaging dispositions), we need to be filled with God's love and grace.

Satan is a bully.

Like the childhood bully who confronted us on the school playground, Satan has no power other than what he can convince us he has. Until we figure out that his tools are only intimidation and the distortion of reality, he wrecks havoc on us   Although he is sneaky and deceptive, he's not at all creative, and uses the same lies on all of us. It is our responsibility to be aware of his tactics.

Satan will keep the upper hand as long as he can isolate us. That's why it's essential that we keep in fellowship with other believers and not isolate ourselves. If we withdraw, we miss opportunities for their ministry of encouragement and their prayers. And when we are feeling wounded and vulnerable, we especially need the body of Christ to intercede for us. At such times, their strong faith becomes our faith. There is power in numbers!

Because of our salvation, our spirits are sealed by the Holy Spirit, and Satan can only attack us in mind, heart (emotions), and body. He simply cannot enter our spirit unless we invite him in. (This is the danger to believers who, without an understanding of the implications, experiment with, or dabble in, astrology, fortune telling, New Age religions, etc.)

Identifying oppression

When I am counseling, there are a number of signs that point me toward oppression as a factor in an individual's overall difficulties. My thoughts turn in that direction when the client
- expresses feelings of being trapped, imprisoned, or in bondage
- expresses despair, hopelessness, or helplessness
- is extremely tired or exhausted for no obvious reason
- experiences prolonged mental confusion or lack of insight
  (mental fog: "I don't get it!")
- says, "Part of me wants to, but part of me doesn't."   (I can hear
  their struggle.)

When our wounds and destructive attitudes are cleansed, we must fill ourselves with God's truth and grace before we can experience healing.

Satan has no power other than what he can convince us he has.

- has understanding and insight followed by inertia (They "get it," but they're stuck.)
- says, "I don't feel like myself."
- or says, "I want to ______, but I don't seem to be able to."

Overall, the impression is of a barrier or strong hindrance to their progress in healing work. Whether the client is simply embedded in their spiritually damaging attitudes or a victim of spiritual bondage, I have, at times, felt as though I was engaged in arm wrestling with the individual.

Seeking prayer support

On occasion, I have encountered clients who exhibit defeatist thinking. They are Christians who come to me saying that they want help, but no matter what exercises or assignments I suggest, they refuse to do the work. Some make excuses for why they "can't" do the work or say, "I really tried to, but I just couldn't do it." Little red flags go up in my mind if this pattern continues.

Karen came to see me following a period of hospitalization for deep depression. During our first few session, she exhibited a very low trust level and did not "engage," or connect, with me in any meaningful way. Although she told me something of her history of sexual abuse, Karen would not do the assignments I gave her, coming back every week with a vague apology and the frequent comment, "Something kept me from doing it." The feeling of discomfort in my spirit became increasingly unsettling, as she continually spoke of not being able to understand what I said or expressed an "I don't care" attitude about some suggestion of mine. I was exhausted when she left my office.

Realizing we needed spiritual "reinforcements," I directed Karen to seek out two or three other women from among her friends to pray for her cleansing from the lies and strongholds, which I felt Satan was using to keep her from working on the issue of her sexual abuse. This cleansing work was absolutely essential before we could begin the work of healing. The change was dramatic. When she returned, Karen no longer exhibited the confusion, forgetfulness, and antagonism with which I had previously "wrestled." She did her grief and forgiveness work with determination and energy, and she is now doing very well.

Spiritual warfare

Satan's goal has always been to keep us out of fellowship with God and deprive us of God's grace, salvation, and the abundant life that begins now and continues into eternity. When we take steps to overcome anything that promotes Satan's goal — including our sin, spiritual woundedness, spiritually damaging dispositions/traits, and addictions — we are engaged in spiritual warfare and need to remember who our enemy is: Satan himself. But our encouragement is that the battle is the Lord's, and victory has already been won through Christ's death, resurrection, and ascension. As Jesus said to His disciples following his resurrection, "All authority in heaven and earth

Satan's goal has always been to keep us out of fellowship with God and deprive us of God's grace, salvation, and the abundant life that begins now and continues into eternity.

has been given to me." (Matthew 28:18) In other words, there is no contest; the ultimate battle is already won. Our confidence that Satan is a defeated enemy should serve us well as we face present-day spiritual conflicts.

As Paul urged the Ephesians, "Finally, be strong in the Lord and in his mighty power. Put on the full armor of God so that you can take your stand against the devil's schemes." (6:10-11) Verses 14 through 17 lists the pieces of that armor:

- <u>Belt of truth</u> - embracing God's truth about His love for us, our relationship with Christ, our worth and value in God's eyes, our God-created individuality, and His purpose for our lives
- <u>Breastplate of righteousness</u> - clothing ourselves in Christ's righteousness because we appropriate His work of cleansing on the cross
- <u>Shoes of the gospel of peace</u> - standing ready to face whatever life brings because of our assurance of God's peace
- <u>Shield of faith</u> - having complete confidence in God's truth and His power
- <u>Helmet of salvation</u> - protecting our mind with the certain knowledge of our salvation through the blood of Christ
- <u>Sword of the Spirit</u> - fighting the enemy with God's written word to counter Satan's lies

My understanding of healing work involves the use of this armor: Affirming our faith in Jesus Christ as our Lord and Savior; studying the Bible with a humble, teachable attitude and journaling about specific Scriptures; worshiping God and having fellowship with other believers; praying for forgiveness and cleansing; trusting confidently in the promises of God; and accepting His healing love to restore our wholeness.

Satanic oppression

Some believers struggle with Satan on another level of conflict — one in which they seem to be more intensely harassed or even singled out for a debilitating, personal attack. Although his tactics seem more cunning in these instances, he is the same defeated foe. While we may not understand why God allows Satan to afflict us, we can be confident that God can — and will — bring us victory and peace.

Release from satanic oppression begins with prayer, and lots of it. The individual who is being harassed should be saturated in prayer by a group of praying friends who call upon God to free the person from Satan's grip. When I feel that one of my clients is dealing with Satanic oppression, I direct them to seek such prayer support from their church family. I also enlist prayer support for myself in my own church.

Shirley fainted in a grocery store one day when she suffered a severe anxiety attack. Her fear was so great that she found it increasingly difficult to leave the safety of her home. Desperately wanting to be healed of this paralyzing fear, she sought my counsel. Nevertheless, after three weeks of meeting with me, Shirley was unable to complete a single assignment or follow one suggestion. It was then that I asked her to enlist prayer support. (While I pray for all my clients, prayer by a body of believers is essential when faced with such strong spiritual harassment — again the power of numbers.)

Although she had been unable to attend her church for some time, she called on women she knew there, sincerely asking for their help. Ten of Shirley's friends prayed with her one afternoon, asking God to cleanse and release her from whatever was keeping her from doing the work that was necessary to find healing. They lifted her up to God in prayer, asking Him to provide direction, cleansing and deliverance. One week later, Shirley was able to go back to church, to eat in a restaurant, and to shop at the grocery store where she had fainted. She worked on her counseling assignments eagerly and examined the deep wounds of her spirit.

Intergenerational dispositions, traits, sin

On occasion I have encountered clients who clearly exhibit a spiritually damaging disposition for which I am unable to detect a triggering event or trend in their history. Patti was overwhelmed by fear, although she had not been victimized or attacked or otherwise had her safety and security threatened. When all efforts to assess her past offered no clues, I focused on a comment she made in one of our early appointments, "I've been frightened as far back as I can remember." Since there was no evidence of a deeply buried event, I asked about her parents' history. I was almost relieved when Patti said that her father had been physically abused by his parents and her mother had been raped as a teenager. Patti's spiritually destructive attitude of fear developed as an extension of her parents' fear. She was, in effect, carrying their wound, tied to it by an intergenerational link.

Oppression from one generation to another can also develop as a result of an ancestor's sin.

Oppression from one generation to another can also develop as a result of an ancestor's sin. This is a Biblical principle: the sins of the father being visited upon a later generation. (Exodus 20:5-6) The good news is that regardless of whether the tie is due to a previous generation's wound, spiritually damaging disposition, or other sin, the link can be broken <u>easily</u> through prayer. The only difficulty is in recognizing what's going on.

Ministry of deliverance

The word "deliverance" summons up images from the movie "The Exorcist" and frightens many churchgoers under their pews. This form of heavy-duty spiritual warfare, though, is sometimes necessary in the face of Satan's extreme tactics. Prayer is our preparation for the battle. Pray for guidance, discernment, wisdom, safety, protection, peace, confidence, and holy boldness. Remember that one of Satan's tactics is intimidation. Standing firmly on the promises of God, we can face this enemy with assurance of victory.

124

This is not a handbook on deliverance ministry. I will tell you that a ten-year-old girl in the mainline church where my husband pastors was seriously oppressed by Satan. With the help of an "army" of praying people and the advice of a pastor for whom such ministry is "routine," a group from our church prayed over the child, and she was delivered.

The physical afflictions, which progressed over a period of weeks from aches, pains, and dizziness to the inability to walk, speak, or do simple arithmetic, were completely healed. What medical science was unable to diagnose or treat, God healed one Sunday afternoon. We may never know with any certainty what brought on this horrible attack, but God graciously nudged the spirits of enough people within the church to realize that deliverance was in order.

Few people experience this degree of oppression. We should not look for Satan "behind every bush" when faced with circumstances that are difficult or painful. Instead, we should seek God's guidance in all matters, resting in the confidence that He will lead our steps.

Front line attack

Quite a few of my clients are spiritually mature, Bible- studying individuals who have been involved in meaningful ministry to others. But because they were experiencing conflict, discouragement, or burnout in their area of service to the body of believers, they sought my counsel. Some were so discouraged that they had withdrawn because of their feelings of unworthiness, shame, and defeat. Even those who recognized that they were being oppressed by Satan saw that as proof that they should not be engaged in ministry.

First, I encourage them to reestablish their fellowship and connectedness with a worshiping body of believers to pray with and for them. Then I explain that the reason they have been singled out by Satan is because they were fighting on the front line of the expansion of the kingdom of heaven. Rather than indicating that they were "bad" people or that their ministry efforts were somehow lacking, the oppression should be recognized for what it really is — a counterattack by an angry enemy who does not want to give up any turf to one of God's warriors!

We should not look for Satan "behind every bush" when faced with circumstances that are difficult or painful.

Assignment
Oppression

1. Make a list of things you would do if you weren't afraid or angry. How would your life change? (This exercise will help you see how much you're blocked by your spiritually damaging dispositions and traits or other source of oppression.)

2. Pray with at least two other people, asking God to reveal your entry point(s) for oppression, that is, to identify specific spiritual wounds, destructive ways of thinking, sins, and/or addictions. Keep in mind that the faith of your prayer partners will be your strength.

3. Ask God in prayer to reveal His plan for showing you your potential for an abundant life.

4. Ask God to reveal what areas still need inner healing in your life.

5. Ask God to remove these destructive attitudes from you and tell Him that you gladly release them.

6. Do something visual to show your release from your spiritually damaging dispositions. Release a balloon or write your destructive attitudes on pieces of paper and burn them. To further represent your cleansing, wash your hands. (Hebrews 10:22)

7. Praise God for the victory over oppression that is yours because of Jesus Christ.

Chapter 16
Spiritual Growth

"Therefore, as God's chosen people, holy and dearly loved, clothe yourselves with compassion, kindness, humility, gentleness and patience. Bear with each other and forgive whatever grievances you may have against one another. Forgive as the Lord forgave you. And over all these virtues put on love, which binds them all together in perfect unity."
Colossians 3:12-14

In the book of Ecclesiastes, King Solomon presents his argument that life lived apart from God is meaningless, but with God there is purpose and a plan for every aspect of life. "There is a time for everything, and a season for every activity under heaven." (Ecclesiastes 3:1) Then follows the familiar listing of times: to be born, to die, to plant, to uproot, to weep, to laugh, to mourn, to dance, etc. Finally, Solomon tells us, "He has made everything beautiful in its time." (Ecclesiastes 3:11)

Seasons of the spirit

When we are living our lives in harmony with God's plan, I believe that there are times in which God's hand moves us into special seasons of our spiritual life for our eternal good and for His ultimate purposes. The seasons of the spirit occur in varying order and are repeated as He directs, but each defines a time of being pulled apart by God from the seemingly ordinary flow of our lives because of His plan for us.

There are times in which God's hand moves us into special seasons of our spiritual life for our eternal good and for His ultimate purposes.

- **Healing** - This is a season of comfort, reassurance and healing of our wounds.
- **Pruning** - Although we may experience some discomfort during the process of being pruned, it is not intended to be a season of suffering. Instead it represents a time in which God calls us to Him for cleansing of our unconfessed sin, repenting of our spiritually damaging dispositions and traits, reordering of our priorities, and taming of our rebellion.
- **Equipping** - This is a season of growing in our awareness of God's presence; in our ability to listen to Him and to respond

Seasons of the Spirit

Healing - God comforts us and heals our wounds when we give them over to Him.

Pruning - God calls us into repentance and cleansing as He "trims" away what offends Him.

Equipping - This is a time of preparation and growing into greater Christlikeness.

Serving - God calls us to share ourselves and our gifts in ministry to others.

There seem to be four distinct seasons, or stages, in which we find our spirit. There is no specific beginning or end; we just move from one to another and, sometimes, back again.

In the original Greek language, Christ's name is "Christos," spelled ΧΡΙΣΤΟΣ. Thus the ΧΡ, or Chi Rho, designate the first two letters of His name. When we allow Christ to live within us, our spirit is more "connected" to Him, and He points us into our spiritual season according to His plan and purposes.

accordingly; and in our knowledge of His plan for us as His children. It is a time of preparation as we grow into greater Christ-likeness and bear a richer harvest of spiritual fruit.
- **Serving** - This is a season of sharing ourselves and our gifts in ministry to others. Like the other seasons, it evolves out of a directive from God.

The material in this book pertains primarily to our seasons of healing and pruning. But it is also important to acknowledge that, as we become increasingly purified, healed and made whole, God wants us to become a blessing to others. For this reason, it is essential that we respond to God's call into our seasons of equipping and serving as well.

Called to Christ-likeness

Since our ongoing appeal from God is to be increasingly Christ-like, we must deliberately pattern ourselves after our perfect model and grow into greater maturity through the enabling of the Holy Spirit. Our humanity puts limits on our understanding, but we must make the effort to become more spiritually alive and open ourselves up to the Spirit's leadership. We do this by moving away from our baby Christian "milk diet" to the mature diet of "spiritual meat." This is the spiritual sustenance that enables us to act on the teachings of the faith — to walk the walk instead of just talking the talk.

Growing into greater Christ-likeness requires that we let go of our former ways and intentionally "put on" Christ.

Growing into greater Christ-likeness requires that we let go of our former ways and intentionally "put on" Christ. Paul's letter to the church in Colosse reminds us that, as Christians, we "have taken off (y)our old self with its practices and have put on the new self, which is being renewed in knowledge in the image of its Creator." (Colossians 3:9,10)

Spiritual sensitivity

As we put on this "new self" more and more each day, our senses become refashioned for enhanced spiritual receptivity. Our awareness of Christ's presence in us increases, and we begin to feel, hear, and see things on another plane — a spiritual plane. A hardened heart cannot hear the Holy Spirit's guidance and comfort, but as we are healed we develop "spiritual ears" and "spiritual eyes" that open us up to receive more of God's holy truth. Likewise, our spiritual vision is perfected as our physical eyes are changed into "spiritual eyes." The points on the following page demonstrate the contrast between our earthly and spiritual perceptions.

As we are healed we develop "spiritual ears" and "spiritual eyes."

Earthly Limitation

1. We see truth that is circumstantial.

2. We listen only to ourselves.

3. We are driven by fear and self-protection.

4. We wonder where God is.

5. We are confused.

6. We see ourselves in terms of performance, behavior, and works.

7. We are in denial and are defensive and filled with shame.

8. We are blaming and judgmental.

9. We feel distanced from God and think He is unknowable.

10. We try to make our own meaning, which leads to self-centeredness.

11. We are filled with despair.

12. We have limited vision and feel powerless.

13. We deny that God created us to be dependent on Him.

14. We feel that God is punishing us.

15. We feel defeated by circumstances and events.

16. We insist on being in control.

Spiritual Openness

1. We see God's truth as unchanging.

2. We listen to God as well as talk to Him.

3. We are fulfilled by a relationship of love, faith, trust, and intimacy.

4. We are aware of God's presence in all things.

5. We receive God's guidance.

6. We see ourselves as God sees us.

7. We hear His truth about ourselves and seek accountability with the body of Christ.

8. We see others as God sees them (using discernment and giving compassion and grace).

9. We have insight about God's loving character.

10. We sense God's purpose, will, and meaning in our lives.

11. We have hope.

12. We have unlimited vision and power through the Holy Spirit.

13. We acknowledge our complete dependence on Christ.

14. We recognize that God has our best interests at heart.

15. We know that all things work together for good.

16. We invite Christ to be in control.

Spiritual openness develops because we earnestly seek God's truth in a relationship with Him. By contrast, those who don't pursue it will be like the other "pew warmers" who come to church yet compartmentalize and minimize their spiritual growth by clinging to a Sunday morning activity instead of the Lord of their lives. Although these baby Christians may even read their Bibles, they don't recognize the God on each page as the One who walks beside them.

Scholarly wisdom of the Bible does not guarantee spiritual openness. When the apostle Paul's vision was restored after his firsthand experience with Christ on the Damascus road, "something like scales" fell from his eyes. (Acts 9:18) Not only could he once again see in the physical realm, but Paul's spiritual eyes were also activated so that he could fully recognize that Jesus Christ was the Messiah promised in Scriptures. The spiritual openness that he developed and his complete confidence in God enabled Paul to carry the gospel to the Gentiles and withstand beatings, stoning, and imprisonment.

Not only is it important that we develop greater spiritual awareness, but we should also seek relationships with people who are spiritually sensitive to help hold us accountable for continued spiritual growth. Likewise we need to act on our spiritual nudges when we feel the Holy Spirit direct us in a specific task.

Gina had been experiencing severe marital problems and was packing her suitcase in preparation for leaving her husband when there was a knock at the door. Gina's neighbor, with whom she had only a casual relationship and had never confided her family struggle, was in prayer when she felt that God told her, "Gina needs a friend." Because she trusted God's promptings, the neighbor was willing to be regarded as a fool when she knocked on the door. Gina, fortunately, recognized her neighbor's visit as an encouragement from God that He knew her pain and promised to meet her needs.

Making amends

As we grow into greater healing and wholeness, we must acknowledge that in the past our words, behaviors, and emotional responses to people have caused them injury. Our increased spiritual sensitivity may improve the situation, but true healing of the relationship is unattainable without our making amends. As Paul advises us, "If it is possible, as far as it depends on you, live at peace with everyone," and "Do not be overcome by evil, but overcome evil with good." (Romans 12:18, 21)

In making amends, we openly acknowledge that we did not perfectly love others. It calls for prayerful reflection and total honesty, for in making amends we are validating what others have experienced because of our imperfect love instead of attempting to justify our attitudes and behaviors. If we are stuck in trying to justify ourselves, we have erected a barrier between us and God's forgiveness, for we are saying, in effect, "I haven't done anything that needs to be forgiven." Amends making can be a very painful experience because it demands honest appraisal of our imperfect love and forces us to see ourselves as we really are. But it contains a lot of healing power as well, for it exposes us to God's forgiveness and grace.

In order to make amends, we must:

- recognize our need to reconcile
- identify our dispositions, traits, and behaviors that have damaged our relationship with God, self, and others
- acknowledge and validate the other person's experience
- take responsibility for the damage we have caused instead of trying to justify our attitudes and behaviors
- apologize
- commit to Christ-like attitudes and behaviors
- accept God's forgiveness
- give Him our guilt

Amends making is often expressed in a face-to-face encounter. But making amends through writing letters can also be quite helpful, since it offers the insulation of distance and allows the other individual time to digest the information and consider if, and how, they might want to respond.

Making amends is a critically important factor in working through marriage difficulties because it validates the experience of pain within the relationship and helps defuse the emotional "bomb" that would otherwise destroy the marriage covenant. By administering healing grace to each other's pain, the marriage partners can step out of their victim/victim roles. Otherwise they experience a perpetual cycle of hurting and being hurt because both have hinged their happiness and fulfillment on their spouse's behavior. But once the relational climate is cleansed, the two individuals can more clearly focus God's healing light on their underlying woundedness.

Notice that in making amends, we are <u>not</u> asking the other party for forgiveness. Whether or not they forgive us is between them and God. As in the forgiveness work described in Chapter 14, there are no guarantees that our efforts to make up for the past will be well received. While making amends sometimes lays the groundwork for reconciliation, the message may also fall on deaf ears. You cannot make the other person O.K. Nevertheless, it is our Scriptural responsibility to set matters straight to the extent that we are able. Otherwise we would miss the healing grace that comes to us because of our obedience and God's forgiveness.

Fruit of the Spirit

As we grow spiritually and allow the Holy Spirit to work in us, we will take on traits that are found in Christ's character and nature. These traits are the fruit of the Spirit: love, joy, peace, patience, kindness, gentleness, goodness, faithfulness, and self-control. (Galatians 5:22-23) Because of our human temperament, some of His qualities come easily, while others require making a deliberate effort. For instance, we may have gratefully received grace but realize that we are not sharing Christ's grace with others. Our goal, then, might be to find ways to express more grace in our interactions with others.

We may recognize that there are times when we can feel and express Christ's peace, for example, but then are sent searching for that peace after some stressful experience. To overcome the effects of the changing needs and circumstances in our lives, we must depend increasingly on the Holy Spirit to work in and through us to form and reflect Christ's character.

Our attention may also be drawn to areas where we need to consciously receive more of Christ before we can demonstrate that trait to others. Bible study and Scripture journaling are helpful in expanding our understanding of such aspects of His character as the comfort of His love when we are feeling rejected by others, or the grace of His forgiveness when we stumble. Once we come to recognize these blessings from Christ and savor their healing quality, we are then able to share the blessing with others.

Sometimes, though, our lives do not demonstrate Christ's nature because there is something blocking the production of that character trait. Self-examination may show us that we are hanging on to unforgiveness, spiritually damaging attitudes, or unhealed woundedness. As a result, we must seek further cleansing, filling, and healing.

Christ Himself tells us, "I am the vine; you are the branches. If a man remains in me and I in him, he will bear much fruit; apart from me you can do nothing." (John 15:5) Production of spiritual fruit, then, grows out of our connectedness to Christ — through prayer, Bible study, worship, and fellowship with other believers. As we grow increasingly Christ-centered, we will produce more fruit. Since He also cautions us, "By their fruit you will recognize them," (Matthew 7:16), our prayer should be that our spiritual fruit production would cause others to see Christ in us.

Deepening our walk

Growth in our relationship with God accelerates as we become more intentional and expressive in our praise and thanksgiving to God for His healing mercy, presence, power, love, and grace. Whether expressed through music, prayer, or spoken words of tribute and honor, we should engage in praise and thanksgiving as part of our everyday spiritual experience. Psalm 29:2 tells us, "Ascribe to the Lord the glory due his name," that is, assign or express to Him the tribute that He is worthy of.

We can also deepen our spiritual walk through expectation — an attitude of anticipation that looks forward to what God has in store for us next and that petitions God with confidence that He will meet our request. The abundant living that we are promised in Scripture is characterized by an attitude of expectancy rooted in God's sufficiency.

Assignment
Spiritual Growth

1. Make a list that includes God, self, and others with whom you need to make amends. Include a brief description of your responsibility in the damage to the relationship and of the ways that you might bring healing to that relationship.

2. Making amends: Based on the list above, do the following amends exercise. Do this **prayerfully**, remembering that you are validating the harmed person's experience rather than justifying yourself.

   a. <u>Identify attitudes/behaviors that have caused damage</u>. This provides recognition of what you have done regardless of what the other person did. Most of these items will focus on attitudes rather than specific behaviors. For example, you may have held resentments against an individual or have not trusted someone. It doesn't matter why you are angry or didn't trust. This exercise is not about justifying our attitudes and behaviors. Instead it leads us into taking responsibility for our choices in how we respond to what life brings us. Remember that our standard is Christ, not the behavior and actions of others or the standard with which we grew up. The question to reflect on is, "How have I fallen short of perfect love?"

   b. <u>Identify the damage to the other person</u>. In order to identify the damage, the phrase to use is "and that must have made you feel . . . ." For example: "I have held resentments against you and that must have made you feel angry, hurt, confused, sad, etc."

   c. <u>Apologize</u>. In short, simple terms, expresses your sorrow for the wound you have caused yourself, God, or others. "I am sorry that/for . . . "

   d. <u>Commit yourself to change</u>. In this step you identify ways in which you will change from this moment forward. For example: "I am sorry that I have held resentments against you. I now choose to forgive you and to be more honest about my hurts when they occur rather than letting them build up over time." It is understood that you will not be perfect in carrying out your commitment, but it is equally understood that you recognize the need for change and are committed to that change.

   e. <u>Accept God's forgiveness</u>. Make this statement: "I choose to accept God's forgiveness and to give Him my guilt." This expresses an understanding that regardless of whether the other person forgives you or not, you are forgiven by Christ and have been given a new start.

   Do this exercise all the way through for <u>each</u> point of tension with each person because the damage and the commitment will be different for each item.

3. Identify two spiritual goals — one in terms of new or enhanced awareness of God's character and the second in terms of the manifestation of that character in yourself. Awareness example: "I need a greater awareness of God's grace." Manifestation example: "I have an awareness of God's grace, but I need to be expressing it in my daily life."

   These goals can change as often as weekly because our needs change. Make yourself accountable to others and seek their support as well. For instance, if your goal is greater awareness of God's grace, then you will ask others how they experience God's grace in their life. If your goal is to express grace, then make yourself accountable to others in your commitment to that goal.

4. You may use the following model when seeking reconciliation. Do this as a written exercise first to help you clarify your understanding.

   a. Make a statement of your desire for reconciliation.

   b. Identify your perception of hurtful events.

   c. Identify your feelings about those events.

   d. Describe the damage to yourself (e.g., a hardened heart caused by resentments).

   e. Make a statement of your decision to forgive.

   f. Identify the conditions that need to be met for reconciliation.

Chapter 17
Gifts from the Wounds

"And we know that in all things God works for the good of those who love him, who have been called according to his purpose." Romans 8:28

"Give thanks in all circumstances, for this is God's will for you in Christ Jesus." (I Thessalonians 5:18) This Scripture always troubled me, for it is extremely difficult to be thankful in all things. It wasn't until I counseled several alcoholics who had learned the secret of gratitude that I was able to understand the verse more completely. My knees would buckle when I heard a recovering alcoholic say, "I am truly thankful for my alcoholism."

In time I understood that what they really meant was they were thankful for the healing to their spirits that came as a result of their alcoholism, which they felt would not otherwise have occurred. While they regretted the pain they had caused, these individuals realized that, in the end, their alcoholism had brought them into a closer relationship with Christ, had resulted in true blessings for their families, and had brought them new friendships. From the deep pit of their wounds, God had brought gifts — gifts they would not have had except for the depth of suffering they endured.

The real essence of the I Thessalonians Scripture, then, is that we should be thankful for Christ's presence, healing, and restoration in all the events of our lives. For although there are times when we feel He is not there, the fact remains that Christ never abandons us. He is always present, weaving the tapestry of life according to His will. No matter how difficult, ugly, or confusing life seems, God always has the final word.

We should be thankful for Christ's presence, healing, and restoration in all the events of our lives.

To fully grasp the nature of God's love, we must remember that He created us with free will. He wants us to love Him, but that love would have no meaning if it were somehow programmed into us. Instead God gave us the freedom to love or reject Him. If we follow His plan, we will come to know Him and our Christ-centeredness will result in abundant living. But God knew that many of His children would choose to go their own way, rejecting Him and wounding each other. He, therefore, enables us to use our various means of self-protection until such time as we are healed and set free in Him. For while we dwell on our past- or present-day suffering, God looks toward our eternal blessing and wholeness in Him.

The oppression of our spiritually damaging dispositions and traits can blind us to God's presence and keep us ignorant of His capacity to meet all our needs. As a result, we may need to accept God's presence and truth as an act of faith and express our gratitude to Him, initially, as a step of obedience. In time, the attitude of gratitude will serve as an antidote to fear, shame, and other destructive attitudes that keep us from grasping God's truths. Then our sincere gratitude will flow freely, and with it will come an awareness of the gift from our wounds.

There will always be gifts from our wounds, <u>at least</u> one gift for each wound . . . guaranteed! Remember in the Biblical account how Job lost everything: possessions, livelihood, children, and health. But after he prayed for the friends who had abused him during his time of loss and suffering, God restored all that he had lost twofold. Job 42:12 says, "The Lord blessed the latter part of Job's life more than the first." Christ does no less for <u>us</u> today.

Turning life around

Jane had been hospitalized because of the damage to her body caused by anorexia, a severe eating disorder. Her weight was down to 75 pounds and she was suffering dehydration before tube feedings were administered. Following her discharge from the hospital, she came to me for continued counseling. Under an umbrella of prayer support from her family and church members, Jane engaged in the healing work with energy and intensity. I sensed in her a real desire to get well and be healed. She came to recognize the truth about herself as God's precious and treasured child and addressed areas of unforgiveness in her life.

A new Jane emerged. She was able to manage a full-time job and became active in her church. Because of her own experience, she had a deep sensitivity to the needs of other young women with eating disorders and began an informal ministry to them. Jane could tell them about God's faithfulness in walking alongside her through each step of her own healing.

Another client, Carolyn, was a highly driven businesswoman but a functioning alcoholic. Her personal life was a disaster, and it was her unhappiness and lack of fulfillment in that area that brought her, quite literally, to her knees. I'll compress the time frame and summarize by saying that she examined her wounds and spiritually damaging dispositions and traits, and sought God's healing and forgiveness. She is now happily married and enjoys a different kind of professional success as a result of her transformation. Under the leadership of the Holy Spirit, Carolyn's destructive attitude of being a "control freak" was tempered and refined into leadership traits, organizational skills, and goal setting abilities.

Children of alcoholics manifest behavior and attitudes that are determined by their way of coping in a highly dysfunctional home. When they experience the healing grace of Christ in their adult years, these spiritually damaging dispositions are transformed. The difference is that their behavior and attitudes are no longer prompted by the pain from which they originally arose. The driven, perfect "hero" child, then becomes a well-organized leader with a high degree of initiative. The fearful, anxious "mascot" child now exhibits a keen sense of humor that defuses stressful situations. The one who suffered abuse demonstrates highly creative or logical thinking that was learned as a way of surviving on the "battlefield."

A miracle-working God

While we worship Him as "Almighty God," we sometimes fail to fully comprehend God's almightiness: that the God who created us and heals us is the God who can also recreate us. It seems that God delights in taking our brokenness and the messes of our lives to orchestrate some present-day miracles.

God delights in taking our brokenness and the messes of our lives to orchestrate some present-day miracles.

In the first five verses of Psalm 103, there is a wonderful passage that says, "Praise the Lord, O my soul, and forget not all his benefits." It then goes on to list these benefits: "who forgives all your sins and heals all your diseases, who redeems your life from the pit and crowns you with love and compassion, who satisfies your desires with good things . . ." To redeem means to set free, rescue, or ransom. When God not only heals us but also gives us gifts from our wounds, it is His way of redeeming our life from the pit and setting a crown on our head.

The nature of the gifts

I have identified five areas in which God gives us gifts from our wounds.

1. Character traits

The first area involves character traits. These distinguishing personal attributes are innate factors that have been shaped by our life experience, including our woundedness, such as in the example above about the adult children of alcoholics. When we examine our coping skills, we will notice that many of our personality characteristics and abilities have come out of past difficulties.

Christ refines and reshapes the elements of our character into attributes with which He can bless us as well as others.

Once Christ heals our wounds, He refines and reshapes the elements of our character into attributes with which He can bless us as well as others. In His hands, stubbornness becomes perseverance and tenacity; stinginess becomes thriftiness; pridefulness becomes confidence; hypersensitivity becomes empathy. Clearly, we would not be the persons we are today apart from our wounds and the resulting gifts.

2. Relationships with people

In the second area, gifts reveal themselves in relationships with people who have brought healing to our lives. When we look back at our lives, we can see that God placed people in our path to serve as ambassadors of His love — to be for us "Jesus with skin." These may have been Sunday school teachers, school teachers, or friends who came alongside us as a reflection of God's grace and care. They provided healing through their presence, words of affirmation and encouragement, acts of service, and touch.

When we look back on the "dry" periods in our lives, we often see how we withdrew from others or insulated ourselves from the ministry of love that was oftentimes only inches away. And in times where we let our defenses down, we can see friendships forged in the fire of suffering that will bless us throughout our lives.

3. Gifts from circumstances or events

Gifts also result from the difficult circumstances or events that shaped our lives through the years. We may not have realized their significance at the time, but, with the clearer vision of retrospect, we can now see that they redirected our life toward healing and wholeness. It may have been a traumatic move across the country that resulted in a greater focus on the importance of family, a job loss that led to a much better employment opportunity, or the grave illness of a child that caused us to examine our priorities in life.

Then there are those circumstances that we simply cannot explain: the book we bought for someone but " misplaced" until we discovered we needed it ourselves; the inner urgency that prompted an old friend to call to see how we're doing — just when we felt we were at the end of our rope. While we may label them as coincidences, they really are "God-incidences," for these events and circumstances have God's fingerprints all over them.

4. Spiritual gifts

The fourth area of gifts comes from God's supernatural transformation and empowerment of our skills and abilities for the benefit and edification of the body of Christ. Spiritual gifts (such as discernment, wisdom, administration, generosity, music, and teaching) may arise out of, or be shaped by, our life circumstances; but under God's enabling, they can be used to bless the lives of others. In fact, we are not fully whole and becoming who God created us to be unless we are using these gifts.

We can see that God placed people in our path to serve as ambassadors of His love.

While we may label them as coincidences, they really are "God-incidences."

Spiritus Sanctus

Spiritus Sanctus — the Holy Spirit — the Spirit of God that lives within us all! Forgiveness rescues us from the attitudes of our spiritually damaging dispositions and traits, allowing for the production of the fruit of the Spirit — the virtues of a Christ-centered life that redirect us from our sinful nature.

Many of our spiritual gifts result from the pain of our past, but they equip us for a ministry of healing. If we have suffered deep emotional or physical pain, God may give us the gift of mercy that we might be able to empathize with hurting people. When God calls us to ministry, He also equips us.

Our connectedness with Christ is essential to the proper sharing of our spiritual gifts. Under the guidance of the Holy Spirit, the use of our gifts will result in blessings for others as well as fulfillment and contentment for us. But if we operate under our own authority instead of His enabling, we will be weighted down with the worries and pains of this world and experience frustration, fear, and anxiety.

5. *Spiritual fruit*

Finally, the fifth area of gifts from our wounds is spiritual fruit: love, joy, peace, patience, kindness, goodness, faithfulness, gentleness, and self-control. (Galatians 5:22-23) These holy attributes are produced in us to increasing degrees when we are Holy-Spirit-controlled instead of self-controlled. For as we allow Him to cleanse, fill, and heal our wounds, God reshapes our character to reflect that of Christ, in whose image He first created us.

God makes use of all the pieces of our lives, not just the periods of comfort and ease. For under the guidance of the Holy Spirit, even the saddest and most frightening times of our wounding can produce gifts with which He can bless us and others as well. Everything can be molded into something of beauty by Christ. Our task is to live life with a thankful spirit that looks <u>expectantly</u> for the fulfillment of His promises.

When God calls us to ministry, He also equips us.

Our task is to live life with a thankful spirit that looks expectantly for the fulfillment of His promises.

142

Assignment
Gifts from the Wounds

1. In your journal, list your areas of woundedness. Beside each one, write about what you learned in the struggle or pain that you now recognize as a positive factor in your life.

2. Name at least one gift in each of the five areas listed below. Continue to have an open heart to the presence of additional gifts as well.

    character traits -

    relationships -

    circumstances/situations -

    spiritual gifts -

    spiritual fruits -

3. Identify ways in which you can increase your spirit of gratitude.

4. Journal "... and this is proof of God's love." In other words, look at your life to find events and circumstances that reflect God's presence, grace, and love. (For example, this morning when you got out of bed, you had breakfast. Be thankful for food.)

5. In your journal, create a "grateful list" every day, recording at least <u>ten</u> items to be thankful for in the following three areas:

   (a) <u>accomplishments</u> for which you feel proud of yourself;

   (b) <u>gifts,</u> such as encouragement and support from others;

   (c) <u>evidence of the presence of God in your life,</u>as revealed through such things as answered prayer or events that clearly reveal God's presence, and through people He has brought to touch your life.

6. If you need help in determining the gifts and graces God has brought from your woundedness, you may want to complete a personality profile and a spiritual gifts inventory. Information about these appears in Appendix C.

Chapter 18
From Suffering to Service

"Praise be to the God and Father of our Lord Jesus Christ, the Father of compassion and the God of all comfort, who comforts us in all our troubles, so that we can comfort those in any trouble with the comfort we ourselves have received from God." II Corinthians 1:3, 4

Turned over to God for His use in blessing others, our suffering can pay dividends! When we struggle on our own, suffering turns us inward, and we become self-absorbed in remembering our own pain. But if we follow God's plan for our cleansing, filling with the Holy Spirit, and healing, we will move steadily from inward reflection to outward service. Each small step on the path to wholeness moves us closer to being used by God for further works of healing. As the Scripture above indicates, comfort was given to us so that we can share it with others. We are not to hoard what we receive from Him.

Comfort was given to us so that we can share it with others.

In the book of Isaiah, which prophesies the coming of Christ, chapter 53 characterizes Him as a suffering servant. Verse five states that "by his wounds we are healed." In other words, a benefit arose out of Christ's suffering; because of His pain, we are made whole. Since we, as Christians, are called to strive for Christ-likeness, it follows then that we must make ourselves available for the beneficial use of <u>our</u> suffering.

We must make ourselves available for the beneficial use of <u>our</u> suffering.

Identify ministry
Sharing the blessing of our healing with those who are broken and wounded begins with determining what it is we have to give. Reflecting on what we have learned about both ourselves and God during the course of our healing and transformation will give us clues to identify our unique ministry. It helps to focus on the special blessing from God that brought healing to our wounded spirit. If we have experienced disappointment and sorrow, for example, the blessing may be our new awareness of the Holy Spirit as the Comforter. We can help someone else get in touch with this comforting presence, which is available to them as well.

Massage My Heart

Massage my heart, O God.
Take it in Your hands and
Give it warmth and life.
Work in Your love
Until it permeates my being.
Massage my heart, O Lord,
Until it beats to the rhythm of You;
Until every cell receives the
Life-giving flow of Your love.
Then will it bleed to others
And they, too, will feel life,
Your life,
Your love, through me.
Massage my heart, O God.

© Melody 1995

We may recognize the powerful testimony we can share with both believers and nonbelievers who struggle alone in their misery. By demonstrating a life transformed by grace and truth, we can bear witness to God's ability to heal and forgive all things. Likewise, a ministry of encouragement may arise from our experience of God's grace and mercy.

Identify recipients

Our ministry may best be received by a particular population or group. Just as our suffering is eased by the knowledge that Christ was "familiar with suffering," we may experience greater effectiveness in our ministry because we have more credibility with those who see the parallel between their own struggle and ours. Our experience also heightens our ability to be truly empathetic with those who suffer as we have. Thus, the particular circumstances of our suffering may lead us to a specific "category" of ministry recipient.

If we suffered hurtful events as a child, we understand how it feels to hurt as a child. From that empathy might grow a passion to minister to children. Our passage through the grieving process after the loss of a loved one may point us toward assisting with a grief support group.

Recognize talents, abilities

In the economy of God's kingdom, He uses all the pieces of who we are to bless others. For this reason we can be sure that our particular talents and abilities will also be reflected in our call to move from suffering to service. If we have excellent teaching skills and also experienced abuse as a child, we might become an effective teacher for children. A person with strong organizational skills who was victimized by a rapist might volunteer her time in the administrative office of a women's center. Tempered by the Holy Spirit, our spiritually damaging dispositions and traits can also be redirected into strengths for ministry.

In the economy of God's kingdom, He uses all the pieces of who we are to bless others.

Called to serve

When we analyze these factors, we will discover a ministry that only we can fulfill. Through it, we are not only given an opportunity to give back to God, but we have another opportunity to see God's enabling hand at work in our lives. It is said that God does not call the equipped, rather He equips the called. When we respond to His healing grace by giving to others in ministry as God directs us, He will faithfully equip us and prosper our ministry.

We are not only given an opportunity to give back to God, but we have another opportunity to see God's enabling hand at work in our lives.

Tricia's life was transformed when God healed her controlling attitude and gave her assurance of her value in His eyes. Reworked in His hands, her perfectionism and obsessive/compulsive drive became organizational abilities and leadership skills. Once Tricia accepted her gifts and graces, she felt drawn into helping people in crisis by serving in lay ministry in her church. Her revitalized relationship with God has enhanced her capacity to be a sympathetic listener.

Suffering to Service

Suffering is a reality in this world, even for Christians. Most of us would agree that our greatest degree of growth occurs during the most difficult times in our lives. Christ intended for our suffering to have meaning by transforming it into a blessing to be shared. Our healing, then, moves us outward to help others and to enrich the body of Christ. How can you best minister to others? With which age group would you be most effective? What talents and abilities has God given you, in particular, that He can use? When we minister to others, we pass on God's healing light.

My friend Bonnie's two children and both of her parents were killed in an automobile accident during the Christmas holidays. Struggling with a kind of pain that is virtually incomprehensible, Bonnie took her brokenness to Christ and allowed Him to hold her and walk with her through the grieving process. She knew from her own experience that there was a need in her community for ministry to people who have lost children through death. Employing her strong administrative and leadership skills, she started a chapter of Compassionate Friends. Through her continuing support of grieving parents, Bonnie demonstrates the principle of comforting others with the comfort she first received from Christ.

In His time

God truly does make all things beautiful in His time. As we saw earlier in Chapter 16, our time to serve is a spiritual season determined by God. It is not based on our decision to serve, nor is it driven by our energy. We must also be careful that we don't allow others to push us into service because they see a need and think we can handle it! Ignoring the demands and expectations of others and our own desire to "do good" or "look good," we must prayerfully consider where God wants us to be. During our season of service, we must continue to be sensitive to the Holy Spirit's redirection into seasons of further healing, pruning, and equipping.

When we give others hope for their own healing, we are transmitting the healing light that we received and reflecting the glory to God. It is a holy work that He accomplishes through us as we model the essence of Christ by using our suffering for the constructive purpose of serving. And, in His hands, the poison of our pain is truly refined into the oil of healing for others.

Assignment
From Suffering to Service

1. Identify and write about your suffering and reconciliation with suffering.

2. Identify your particular talents, abilities, and personality traits which, in combination with your suffering, will benefit others. Appendix D includes questionnaires designed to help you know yourself better and use your talents for Christ and His church. Take time to begin completing these questions.

3. Your suffering means little if done is isolation. Write about ways that your suffering can benefit others and edify the body of Christ.

4. Identify particular groups or persons for whom the experience of your suffering would be most beneficial.

5. Develop a plan and a timetable to share your suffering and reconciliation with that suffering. Begin today.

Chapter 19
Love

"No, in all these things we are more than conquerors through him who loved us. For I am convinced that neither death nor life, neither angels nor demons, neither the present nor the future, nor any powers, neither height nor depth, nor anything else in all creation, will be able to separate us from the love of God that is in Christ Jesus our Lord." Romans 8:37-39

Love makes us whole. It is the nourishment by which we become the Christ-like individual God created us to be. Unless we give and receive love, we cannot be fully ourselves, for love feeds our spirit and brings vitality and growth to our life. Without it, we become sick — emotionally, mentally, and spiritually — because without love we lose our true sense of self. Not only do our wounds keep us from growing in our capacity to love, our methods of self-protection block the free flow of love in either direction. No healing therapy is complete apart from Christ's love because it is only through receiving and modeling this love that we can become healthy and whole.

Our goal in life is to learn to love as Christ loves us.

Our goal in life, then, is to learn to love as Christ loves us. Since love is a spiritual quality, not a personality characteristic, we must allow our spirit to be shaped and conformed by His Holy Spirit. Thus, unconditional, sacrificial, and inspirational love develops only out of an intimate relationship with Christ. The people who came in contact with the disciples noted how these men loved, for they sensed the selfless nature of the disciples' love. We, like the disciples, will demonstrate that love as we increasingly spend time with our Savior and welcome the interior ministry of the Holy Spirit.

Love is a spiritual quality.

As creatures of God made in His image, our two greatest needs are to love and to be loved. In fact, our need to love is just as compelling as the need to be loved. This twofold nature of love is implied in the "new command" given to us by Christ: "Love one another. As I have loved you, so you must love one another." (John 13:34) Just as God enables us to do whatever He calls us to do, He makes it possible for us to love others as Christ loved us: "God has poured out his love into our hearts by the Holy Spirit, whom he has given us." (Romans 5:5b) We, then, become vessels through which that

We can love others only to the extent that we have allowed Christ to love us.

love can be given to others. The problem is that our vessel becomes blocked by the spiritually damaging dispositions and traits we adopt to protect our wounded selves. Until we are completely healed, we can love others only to the extent that we have allowed Christ to love us — and that is limited by our foundational experience of love.

Love satisfies needs of the spirit

While movies and songs would lead us to believe otherwise, love is not an animal response to hormones nor is it, simply, the full bloom of affection. Philosophers and poets have written volumes about love, but no description surpasses what the apostle Paul wrote in his first letter to the Corinthians: "Love is patient, love is kind. It does not envy, it does not boast, it is not proud. It is not rude, it is not self-seeking, it is not easily angered, it keeps no record of wrongs. Love does not delight in evil but rejoices with the truth. It always protects, always trusts, always hopes, always perseveres. Love never fails." (I Corinthians 13:4-8a)

If you compare this passage to the list of our needs of the spirit (safety, security, value, acceptance, nurturing, understanding, forgiveness, and belonging), you can see that unconditional love satisfies those needs.

"Love continuum"

When our spiritual needs are not met, our understanding of love can become incomplete or distorted. Look at the following "love continuum," a line graph in which 0 percent is the total absence of love and 100 percent is Christ's pure, unconditional love. In other words, at 0 percent, no spiritual needs are met, and at 100 percent, all spiritual needs are fulfilled.

If, for example, we were loved at only the 10 percent level as we were growing up (i.e., 10 percent of our needs were met), we will respond in one of these three ways:

1. We may say, "<u>This is all love is. I don't expect any more than this from others</u>." Victims of abuse are often given a mixed message following episodes of abuse (e.g., "You know your daddy loves you.") With or without such verbal misrepresentation of love, the abuse itself can so distort a victim's concept of love that they later marry an abusive person. Although the individual suffered terribly, the abuse characterizes what they expect to receive from one who "loves" them.

2. If we see that other people are being loved differently (more) than we have experienced, we may decide, "<u>If that's what love is, then I'm not loved</u>," which leads us to feeling shame for our unlovableness.

3. Another possibility is that we examine our past and decide, "<u>They loved me to the capacity they were capable of. With God's help, I'll do better</u>." This is the healthy choice, for it involves forgiving others for their inability to love us more and frees us to grow in our own capacity to give and receive love.

Limited capacity to love

Since our understanding of the nature of love is drawn from our personal experience of love as wewere growing up, our capacity to give love and receive love from others is shaped by that experience. Being loved in a way that did not give us safety, security, value, acceptance, nurturing, understanding, forgiveness, and belonging, results in our having a flawed concept of what love is all about. It's as though the deprivation of any aspect of unconditional love has left us "love-disabled" in that area.

Our understanding of the nature of love is drawn from our personal experience of love as we were growing up.

Our ability to receive all that Christ has for us — including His love — is also blocked by this early shaping of our understanding of love. If our expectation is that Christ is going to love us at the 10 percent level, then we only receive from Him at the 10 percent level. Likewise, if we had a parent who demanded perfection as a condition of love and acceptance, it is likely that we will expect the same conditional acceptance from God and will mistakenly believe He will love us only if we're perfect.

And since it is Christ's love to us that we pour out to others, if our experience has limited us to receiving only a fraction of His love, that is all we have to pass on. We cannot give what we have not received. If we have allowed Christ to love us in only four out of the eight areas of need, we can only love in those four ways, since that's all we have to give. If we have received value, safety, security, and belonging, for example, but have failed to accept nurture, forgiveness, acceptance, and understanding, then we cannot give others nurture, forgiveness, acceptance, and understanding.

We cannot give what we have not received.

Vulnerability

Love is characterized by vulnerability, which is rooted in our ability to trust God. Without the foundation of that trust, we are afraid to risk being open to others. We misunderstand the issue of trust and find ourselves wounded over and over when we continually trust others and rely on them to supply our spiritual needs. Our only need is to trust God. (Proverbs 3:5- 6; Psalm 9:10) Nowhere in the Scriptures is there any command to trust others. The Scriptures do encourage us to be vulnerable, to be ourselves without reservation, and to share our lives with others — but God gives us no guarantee that we will not be hurt in the process. Our Christian walk is not about safety and living life free from pain; it is about living our lives openly and with vulnerability.

Christ took our sins to the cross in order to make a relationship with God possible. While God wants all of His children to respond to His love and call to repentance, He gave us free will to accept or reject His love. Christ knew that many would reject the plan of salvation. At any time He could have called on the power of God to stop the crucifixion, yet He chose not to protect Himself.

And even after His terrible suffering and death, He continues to be vulnerable, for His death did not make us perfect. We still fail in our Christian walk, and, although Christ is disappointed when we do, He doesn't give up on the relationship. He continues to freely share His life with us in order to demonstrate the depth of His love by providing the second chances that are the "loopholes of grace." His continuing to walk with us and love us is our example of vulnerable, patiently waiting love.

Passion

Another characteristic of love is passion — a zealous, fervent devotion that is characterized by "not worrying about the cost." It is about love expressed in the absence of fear, for we cannot have passion without letting ourselves be vulnerable. A wonderful example of this is the love Mother Teresa felt for the impoverished people of India. Driven by her passion for them, she worked among the dying poor — never stopping to consider the cost to herself, emotionally or physically. Her whole life was spent in selfless, unconditional love and service to a people whom the world overlooked.

Many of us never experience this long-term, committed devotion in our lives because we are unwilling or afraid to risk. We hide and protect ourselves instead of opening ourselves up to feel and act passionately. As a result of our clinging to caution and control, we experience a loss of self, and our spirit is damaged because we can only love conditionally.

Regaining passion means coming alive to all that God has created us to be, and it begins, first and foremost, with having a passion for Christ. Only from that relationship can we experience the kind of freedom in our love that drives away our fears and results in expressions of compassion. The capacity to love passionately grows out of faith in God's love and a willingness to let Christ direct our lives according to His will, not our own. As a result we can give up control of our lives and quit demanding protection — for passion knows that it is far better to have the comfort of God's presence than the illusion of confidence based on predictability.

Servanthood

The next characteristic of love is servanthood, which is the application of love that grows from our vulnerability and passion. All too often, we try to serve through an act of our will, and as a result, we become burned out and feel empty and dry. We try to "be good" by doing the "right" things. While servanthood apart from Christ can become co-dependency, true servanthood comes from a healthy fullness in our own spirits. We are enabled to minister to others naturally, then, because our servanthood is an overflowing of God's love in our lives.

When we become a partner with Christ in healing the spiritual wounds of others, we fulfill our greatest calling of servanthood. Many times in the

Church, though, we are co-wounders rather than co-healers because we are unaware of the needs of others and respond without sensitivity.   It is only when we recognize the unmet needs of others that we can minister Christ's comfort, encouragement, and healing.

This is not to say that we should be mind readers or detectives who try to ferret out what others need. On the contrary, each of us is responsible for sharing our needs with others in ways that allow them to minister to us. Co-healing is about expressing grace, and we can best be grace-givers in our relationships with others when we are honest about our own needs, struggles, successes, and failures. Stripped of our pretenses, we can kneel down to serve our fellow human beings in love and grace.

Spiritual gifts

Love also involves the sharing of our spiritual gifts. Because God has called us to a lifetime of vulnerability, grace, forgiveness, love, and servanthood, He also equips us with spiritual gifts. These gifts are given to us for the edification and encouragement of others. They are also to be used for comfort and ministry. None of us is without spiritual gifts. We need only to discover what our gifts are and to use them as Christ directs us. An assignment at the end of this chapter will help you identify your spiritual gifts.

Because many of us are driven by guilt and fear, we sometimes serve in ways that do not match our gifts. For instance, we may be teaching Sunday school, yet feel very little fulfillment in that role. The underlying issue might be that our gifts are better suited toward hospitality or mercy rather than teaching. Continuous frustration may be a sign that we are attempting ministry in an area where we have not been gifted.

Empowered by Christ's love

In the Scripture cited at the beginning of this chapter (Romans 8:37-39), Paul says that nothing can separate us from God's love. Among the various things he enumerates as being unable to stop the flow of love through Christ to us, Paul mentions "the present" and "the future." Although "the past" is not on the list, I believe we would not be stretching Biblical truth if we assume that nothing in our past can separate us from Christ's love either.

No matter what we've experienced in life, no matter what we've done or not done, Christ's love has always been present and flowing in our direction. Even our inability to fully receive His love does not stop its flow. When we acknowledge and receive that love and its healing power, we will be able to pass it on in vulnerable, passionate servanthood and ministry.

Denise did just that. She would not have thought it possible when she first came to see me. All she knew then was that she was depressed about her life and the excessive weight that sapped her strength and added to her self-loathing. The victim of physical, sexual, and spiritual abuse, Denise was oppressed with shame, bitterness, and unforgiveness. She wanted desperately to feel differently about herself and about life, so she took her assignments

None of us is without spiritual gifts. We need only to discover what our gifts are and to use them as Christ directs us.

Even our inability to fully receive Christ's love does not stop its flow.

very seriously — journaling about her feelings and Scripture passages; praying and asking friends to pray for her; forgiving others, herself, and God; and stepping out in faith to believe what God's word said about her and her value to Him.

Not only did God heal her woundedness and minister to her needs of the spirit, He transformed Denise's wound for His glory and to enable her to spread His love. Today she is a minister and leads Bible studies for women and couples. Because she feels a passion for helping others as she was helped, she is willing to be vulnerable and tell the story of her own struggle. By not counting the cost, Denise can share the hope we all have because of Christ.

Yoked to Christ

Christ tells us, "Come to me, all you who are weary and burdened, and I will give you rest. Take my yoke upon you and learn from me, for I am gentle and humble in heart, and you will find rest for your souls. For my yoke is easy and my burden is light." (Matthew 11:28-30)

These verses don't make much sense to us if we don't understand the function of a yoke. Oxen (as well as mules and other draft animals) are often trained to perform their work by using a connecting crossbar to link an inexperienced animal with one that is highly skilled. When the "novice" ox starts to turn in the wrong direction, the yoke provides the necessary tug of redirection on the proper path so that it doesn't fumble through a series of mistakes. After repeated realignment of its steps to the movement of the experienced ox, the once self-directed animal moves in complete harmony with the other.

A yoke can also serve as a device to divide the weight of a load, whether carried or pulled. You may recall pictures of people carrying two buckets by fastening them to a wooden yoke resting across their shoulders. In shifting the weight of the filled buckets to the individual's shoulders, the burden of effort in carrying the load is reduced. The yoke that pairs and coordinates the movement of animals also divides the work effort required for pulling the load to which they are hitched. The weaker animal thus benefits from the superior strength of its yoke-mate.

When we are yoked to Christ, we benefit from both His guidance and His strength.

When we are yoked to Christ, we benefit from both His guidance and His strength because we allow the Holy Spirit to come along side as well as dwell within us. We can then become all that God created us to be because He teaches us how to do it. And when we struggle with the weight of hurt and disappointment, we can shift our burden to His strong shoulders so that we can continue to walk forward in faith.

As we receive, experience, and express Christ's love, we receive the greater healing.

The yoke that Christ offers us is His love — love that both guides and enables us — love that forgives and takes away the burden of oppression — love that heals and teaches us how to love. And as we receive, experience, and express Christ's love, we receive the greater healing.

What color are your wings?

When we give God control of our lives and allow Him to heal our wounds and meet the needs of our spirit, we find ourselves, at last, on that marvelous path to wholeness. The butterfly, one of the symbols for the resurrected Christ, depicts the joy of our transformation as we follow His plan for our lives. Like this little butterfly, we are transformed and released into being all that God created us to be in Him. Do your wings reflect the glorious colors of Christ — or your <u>own</u> paint job?

Assignment
Love

1. Identify ways to become more vulnerable in your life.

2. Co-healing exercise: Go to a person that you feel close to and do the following exercise with each other:

    a. <u>Speaker</u>:   "My greatest unmet need is _______ because . . ."
      <u>Response</u>:   "I am sorry that your need for ______ was not met."

    b. <u>Speaker</u>:   "A way you can meet my need is ______ (specify)"
      <u>Response</u>:   "I will meet your need for _______ by _______ ."
      (Repeat an understanding of the request made.)

    c. <u>Speaker</u>:   "I choose to accept your ______ (unmet need, such as acceptance) even when you fail me." (This is a recognition that others are not perfect, but that their intent is to provide healing for us.)
      <u>Response</u>:   "I want to give you God's blessing of __________ ."
      (Share with them Scripture or prayer or your understanding of God's _______ .)

Each person is to be both speaker and responder. This can be very healing for both persons because it requires vulnerability.

3. Identify the "holes" in your capacity to love and seek ways to increase your capacity to love.

4. Romans 5:5 says that God pours His love into us. In I John 4:11-12 we read that since God loves us, we also ought to love one another, and that if we love one another, God lives in us and His love is made complete in us. Identify ways that you are blocking God's love being poured into you and ways that you are blocking God's love flowing toward others. Ask God to remove these blocks so that you may be a vessel for His love and grace.

5. Identify your spiritual gifts. You can do this through asking others what they think your gifts are and by asking God to reveal them to you. Spiritual gifts tests are also available that can help you identify them as well. (See Appendix C.) Identify ways that your spiritual gifts can edify the body of Christ, the church, and begin today to use them accordingly.

Epilogue

It is less than a week before Thanksgiving as I write this. I have just returned from having lunch with a former client and her husband. God never ceases to amaze me! Quite honestly, I didn't want to meet with Jane and John; I couldn't see what purpose it would serve. But now I know that if I had not talked with them, I would have missed one of God's richest blessings for my life.

About eight years ago, I was Jane's therapist when she was a patient in a psychiatric hospital. She was 18 years old at the time and quite a "toot," testing limits and pushing the edge at every opportunity. To say that she was a challenge is quite an understatement. She was a "street wise" girl who had been living the life of the streets since she was 15.

I particularly remember two different incidents while she was in the hospital. First, she was the only client I ever had who brought a .357 pistol with her. She had smuggled it in her audiotape case. When we discovered she had it, we obviously did some fast talking. She insisted she had brought it to protect herself, not to harm others. Because she had been dealing drugs and had crossed someone, Jane was afraid he would come after her at the hospital.

In the second incident, I was sitting on her bed, trying to reach this child by explaining how much God loved her, regardless of what she had done. Jane began to cry and then to get mad. She was angry at herself for the tears because she saw them as a sign of weakness. Stubborn, angry, rebellious, self-sufficient, and "in control," Jane was also hurting, afraid, and filled with feelings of shame and inadequacy. After leaving the hospital, she moved to another city because of all her problems — legal, drug dealers, etc. Once again, she was running as fast as she could — from others, from her pain, from herself, from God.

I did not hear from Jane again until this past year, when she began to call me on a weekly basis, wanting to see me. It seems she had been in a near fatal car accident five years ago. She suffered a closed head injury that had left its scars on her life, but it had also left her with many blessings as well. When she called on the phone, I could detect a softness and a sweetness of spirit that had not been there years before. Still, when she called saying she wanted to see me, I was unsure of what to expect. I felt strange and awkward, not knowing what I should say to her. Finally, and reluctantly, I agreed to meet her and her husband for lunch.

I cannot begin to tell you the blessing I received today! We sat down for lunch and spent two hours visiting. The time just flew by! First, they told me about the accident. Jane was determined to go see a friend that Halloween night. At first, her boyfriend, John (now her husband), asked to take her. Then, when she refused, he suggested that he at least follow her since he knew that she was not a good nighttime driver, that she would probably be speeding, and that she was in no condition to drive. After arguing for three hours, Jane drove away and later had the terrible wreck.

She suffered a closed head trauma, but a small cut — her only external injury — delayed emergency surgery to release the pressure on her brain. Since Jane was a free bleeder, it took four hours for the hospital staff to stop the flow of blood from what should have been a minor wound. By that time, her brain had quit swelling, and there was no longer any need for the surgery. It is likely that the effects of the head trauma would not have been as severe if they had been able to perform the surgery when she was first brought in, yet the small cut may have saved her life, since the surgery could have resulted in hemorrhaging.

The head injury left Jane in a coma, with absolutely no response for three months. The doctors gave little hope, saying that, if she survived, she would probably be in a vegetative state. When she did come out of the coma, she was moved to a rehabilitation hospital, where she remained for one year. She did not talk or walk for nearly two years. From the night of the accident, John went to the hospital every day.

Today when I saw her, Jane's speech was good, and she is able to walk with the help of a walker. Prior to the accident she had been right-handed, but because of the brain injury, she has had to learn to use her left hand. She is able to be fairly self-sufficient, and her next hurdle is to learn to drive again!!

The stubbornness that had been there years before had been tempered by the Holy Spirit and transformed into the determination that has enabled her to persevere through the rehabilitation process. Imagine two years of not being able to walk or talk — without giving up. Her stubbornness-turned-determination made me smile at God's sense of humor and goodness, for He used it for His glory and her benefit!

As I sat there listening to their story, I kept saying to Jane, "You really are a miracle. Do you know that?" And she would respond confidently, "Yes, I know." Of course, she was a miracle physically because she was able to do far more than was ever thought possible, but the greater miracle was the spiritual healing that had taken place. I felt awed by this young woman's spirit of gratitude that had replaced her anger. Years ago, Jane had resisted and denied her need for love. Today she overflows with love, being able to receive and to give love as well. She exhibited such a sweet spirit, it was a delight and joy to be with her. Her softness and a kindness were a confirmation to me that the spiritual healing is the greater healing.

I was also deeply impressed by the sacrificial love of her husband, who has gone through tremendous grief and loss. John, now 28 years old, is completely devoted to Jane. It's not a "Pollyanna" attitude, for he was absolutely candid with me when he shared his frustrations. He told me that he often feels more like a 50-year-old because of all that he has been through in his short life. For more than a year he drove one hour each way, both before and after work, to see Jane. That's four hours of extra driving every day. Finally, he moved closer to the hospital.

John said he had always loved Jane and wanted to marry her, but she was too independent and self-sufficient. She didn't need or want to be tied down. Then, after the accident, he had to wait again for her to even begin to understand what marriage meant. They married approximately three years ago. Although John is very attentive to her, he is not overly protective of her. He encourages Jane and challenges her. After our lunch, he was going to take her ice skating, because she had once been a great ice skater!

One of the most poignant moments in our time together was when John said that, although it had been hard, he did it because he loved her. He also said he hoped someone would do this for him if he needed it. At which point, Jane very firmly stated that, if necessary, she would take care of him until the day she died. Then John looked at me and said, "I can't imagine our not being together because she is a part of me." I was awed at such mature and passionate love.

As they talked of the struggles and frustrations during these years, there was also an ongoing theme of the many prayers from their families' churches and friends that had uplifted them. John gave credit to prayer for the healing that had taken place.

Most of Jane's memory from before the accident has been lost. She laughed about the things I told her had happened during those few weeks in the psychiatric hospital — but she didn't remember them. How was it, then, that she remembered <u>me</u> at all? Yet, John said I was one of the first people she wanted to contact as soon as she was able. Since I had moved to another city, it had taken awhile to locate me.

Clearly, it was a time where Christ had used me to reach her. I was again humbled that when the Holy Spirit has His way in me, I never know what benefits and blessings occur to me and to others. I was moved to tears when I realized the providence of God. We may never know nor understand why things happen in our lives, but I am confident that God's will and purpose will prevail if we let Him. From the tiny cut, to Jane's spiritual change, to the sacrificial love of her husband, to the blessings in my life, I am convinced of God's goodness and mercy and grace.

You see, Jane's greatest need was to feel loved — to be able to give and receive love so that she might be all that God created her to be. Is she completely physically healed? No. But today Jane stands as one whose deepest needs have been met and who serves as a testimony to the greatest healing of all — the love and grace of Jesus Christ.

The Butterfly

About midway into the writing and illustrating of this book, the subject of the butterfly came up in reference to it being a symbol of Christ's resurrection. Over the ensuing weeks, I began to formulate an idea for an illustration using the butterfly to accompany the concept of our own transformation into a new creature and Marty's probing question, "What color are your wings?" I was also working with Marty regarding the choice of color and layout for the book cover.   It was at this point that she requested a small butterfly on the back cover to tease the reader's curiosity, as the book presents the concept of transformation from brokenness to healing through our risen Savior.

I began to explore various mediums and decided upon colored inks because of their beautiful gloss and intensity. It took practice as these inks tend to be runny and are very permanent. They stimulated my creative bent, since you can add numerous things to the ink and to the paper itself in order to achieve a variety of unique effects. Nearing the end of the second day of layering color on a particular piece, I dropped 10 or 12 blobs of oil in the center of what I imagined to be the front cover. Then I followed that with about 10 squirts of opaque white ink. The ink resisted the oily surface and seemed to have no idea of where to go. I wadded up some waxed paper, laid it over the oil and white ink, covered the entire wet painting with a sheet of plastic to promote more even drying, laid a book on top of the waxed paper, and set the whole thing out of the way to dry.

Three days later, I pulled everything off. I was dumbstruck when there, before me, was a butterfly! Wet paper, very thin, wet ink, oil, wads of waxed paper, and a book do NOT equal a butterfly. I knew that God had been playing with my ink, and He did what I <u>never</u> could have done. You've never seen three more startled and freshly inspired women as Marty, Kay, and me.

The evening after I showed the cover art to Marty, I had one of those jarring, unpleasant experiences with someone — one that is difficult to think about and even harder to talk about. I knew I wasn't handling it very well and decided to drop by Marty's office to see if she could help me come to terms with what had happened. Unfortunately, she had back-to-back client sessions and was unable to see me. Discouraged and crying, I was walking across the parking lot to my car when something on the pavement caught my eye. Leaning down to get a better look, I was astonished to see a little butterfly. His wings were folded and he was obviously wounded, but he was still alive. I picked him up gently and continued to my car as he clung to my finger.

After I settled into the car, he rested in my hand and opened his wings as though to show off his beautiful colors. A leg was missing, a couple of pieces of his left wing as well, and his antennae trembled every few moments. His wings were a beautiful brown with orange hatch marks on the front edges, light tan borders on the lower edges, and six wonderfully colored "eyes."

"Wow, a butterfly!" it finally dawned on me. Here I was, having an up-close-and-personal encounter with a butterfly when the past week had been filled with "butterfly this" and "butterfly that."

"What does it mean, God?" I asked through the steady flow of tears and runny nose. "Help me here, Lord. The butterfly . . . symbol of the resurrection. What does the resurrection have to do with <u>me</u>?"

And suddenly the answer came, so very simply: "I am the resurrection and the life. He who believes in Me should not perish but have everlasting life. I'm here, Joy. I'm <u>always</u> here for you. I'm here when Marty can't be. I'm here when friends can't be. Lean on ME."

Then I remembered what Marty had told me again and again: "Crawl up into His lap and let Him hold you and comfort you."

When the tears finally stopped, I marveled that if I had called Marty ahead of time and found out that she was booked all afternoon, there would have been no reason to be on this parking lot. And even if Marty had been able to see me, I might have returned to my car too late to see the butterfly. Then I looked out at the cloudy, cold November sky and realized this wasn't exactly a butterfly sort of day.

I can't think of another time in my life when God has been so "in my face." He has been "all over" this book as well as my life since my involvement in it began. In fact, each of us has had wonderful experiences of God's hand of leading and blessing as our work proceeded in His enabling power.

Mr. Butterfly rode home with me, with wings folded, and lived until the following evening. For those interested, I found him in my butterfly book. He was a Junonia Evarete. Studying him closely under my magnifying light, I found his underside to be even more beautiful than the top. Now isn't that just like something our Lord would think of?

Thank you, Lord, for that little butterfly to remind me that you are <u>always</u> there for us. One day, like the butterfly, I'll be completely transformed, too. Thank you for wonderful friends, for all that you've blessed us with. Thank you for an end to the tears that day. Thank you, Jesus!

Joy

Needs of the Spirit
Definitions and Scriptures

<u>Safety</u>

To be free from danger; protected and guarded from harm; free from fear of abandonment or rejection

Romans 8:37	Deuteronomy 33:27	Hebrews 10:19-23
Psalm 91	Proverbs 18:10	John 5:24
Romans 8:1	Jude 24-25	

<u>Security</u>

To be assured of safety; confident of being kept safe; safekeeping; characterized by order, stability and consistency

I John 1:9	Ephesians 1:13-14	Hebrews 6:17-20
Proverbs 3:26	I John 5:14-15	II Corinthians 1:21-22
Deuteronomy 7:9	Psalm 145:13	I Thessalonians 5:23-24

<u>Value</u>

To be appreciated for importance, desirability, worth, or merit; regarded highly; esteemed; considered to be important and special; significance; precious; priceless

Luke 12:6-7
Luke 12:22-34 (especially v. 24)
Luke 15 - Parables of the Lost Sheep and the Lost Coin

<u>Acceptance</u>

To be esteemed; received favorably; regarded as right; received gladly and willingly; seen as satisfactory and sufficient; respected; confirmed; unconditional approval for who we are, not for what we do or don't do

Ephesians 1:5-6 (In King James "He hath made us accepted in the beloved . . . ")

Psalm 6:9	Romans 15:7	Acts 10:34	Romans 3:28

Nurturing

To be nourished and sustained; cared for and fed; provided for; cultivated; helped to grow and develop; supported; given tender loving care; being fostered and furthered; mothered; given encouragement, comfort, affection and care; guided with direction and strength

Proverbs 22:6	Deuteronomy 32:10-11	Isaiah 40:11
Isaiah 58:11	Deuteronomy 8:3	Psalm 32:8
John 14:26	John 4:10, 13	John 6:35
John 7:38	Philippians 4:19	I John 2:27
Matthew 4:4	I Peter 5:7	Revelation 21:3-4
Revelation 21:6-7	Revelation 22:1-2	Revelation 22:7

Understanding

Aware of the meaning of; recognizing the existence and meaning of with a sympathetic attitude; compassionate and sympathetic reception; comprehending; having perception and discernment of needs

Psalm 119:104	Psalm 139:1-16	Genesis 2:7	Proverbs 23:23
Psalm 103:13-14	Psalm 8:3-9	II Corinthians 5:21	Proverbs 15:32
II Corinthians 12:9	Romans 5:8	Hebrews 4:14-16	Proverbs 4:7
Proverbs 3:5-6			

Forgiveness

Pardon from punishment or redress; excused of fault or offense; absolved from payment of debt; freed from the consequences of; pardoned without the holding of resentment; given grace and redemption

Psalm 130	II Chronicles 7:14	Isaiah 55:7	Ephesians 1:7
Micah 7:18	Nehemiah 9:17	Matthew 6:14	Colossians 1:13-14
Mark 11:25	Colossians 3:13	Acts 10:43	Ephesians 4:32

Belonging

To be a part of; to fit in with another; having a close, secure relationship; having a sense of connection; having a place of intimate association

John 15:18-19	Romans 1:5-6	Romans 7:4	Isaiah 43:1
Galatians 5:24	Job 41:11	Ezekiel 18:4a	Jeremiah 1:5
John 8:47	Romans 12:4-5	I Corinthians 6:19-20	Isaiah 49:16
I Peter 2:9-10	John 10:1-16	John 10:27-30	

Appendix B
Feelings Vocabulary

In order to talk about your feelings — both "positive" and "negative" — and write about them in your journal, you may need to increase your feelings vocabulary. While the words in this section do not represent a complete list of feelings terminology, you may find them helpful in putting labels on your feelings. Men know what they <u>think</u> about things and situations, but they seem to struggle with recognizing their feelings more so than women do. It is my hope that a presentation of such terminology will be useful for anyone trying to get in touch with what their feelings are telling them about the wounds to their spirit.

Five main emotions
There are five main categories of emotion, with all other feelings terminology describing the various ranges of intensity.

mad:	irritation	➡	rage
happy:	amused	➡	delirious
sad:	blue	➡	depressed
fear:	anxious	➡	panic
hurt:	injured	➡	traumatized

Pleasant or positive feelings:

optimistic	happy	alive	good
confident	reassured	playful	calm
free	joyous	energetic	reassured
sympathetic	delighted	liberated	at ease
interested	overjoyed	optimistic	comfortable
satisfied	elated	impulsive	pleased
affirmed	blessed	capable	encouraged
accepting	ecstatic	excited	content
fortunate	glad	enthusiastic	secure
valued	cheerful	thrilled	hopeful
relaxed	thankful	devoted	comforted
serene	validated	honored	empowered
grateful	loving	sympathetic	brave
important	passionate	eager	daring
refreshed	considerate	earnest	challenged
lucky	affectionate	inspired	hopeful
admiration	sensitive	determined	free
thoughtful	kind	generous	understanding
giving	trusting	forgiving	aware
receptive	respected	helpful	honest
secure	appreciated	renewed	whole

Unpleasant or negative feelings:

angry	depressed	embarrassed	hopeless
enraged	disappointed	unpopular	untrustworthy
hostile	ashamed	disillusioned	desperate
annoyed	powerless	cheated	insecure
unappreciated	diminished	distrustful	demeaned
hateful	guilty	lost	manipulated
unpleasant	dissatisfied	discouraged	trapped
offensive	miserable	uneasy	ashamed
bitter	disgusting	pessimistic	rejected
resentful	terrible	tense	hurt
ugly	despair	incapable	abused
incensed	overwhelmed	sad	unloved
infuriated	doubtful	unimportant	worthless
defensive	uncertain	afraid	defeated
rebellious	confused	helpless	alone
abandoned	dishonored	isolated	violated
dependent	humiliated	frustrated	unattractive
failure	ignored	stupid	weak
misunderstood	immature	betrayed	nagged
critical	smothered	undeserving	resistant
stubborn	incompetent	pressured	neglected

Appendix C

Personality Plus is a personality profile created by Fred Littauer.

Copies may be ordered from:

CLASS Book Service
4065 Oceanside Blvd., Suite R
Oceanside, CA 92056
(619) 631-1604
For credit card orders,
call toll-free (888) 678-1235

Discovering Your Spiritual Gifts: A Personal Inventory Method,
by Kenneth Cain Kinghorn

This booklet presents one of several approaches to identifying your spiritual gifts. It is a publication of the Francis Asbury Press/Zondervan.

Appendix D

Personal Insights

The exercises on the following pages will help you formulate a plan for using your talents for Christ and His church.

Knowing Your Heart - Matthew 6:19-21

1. Describe the church issues, ministries, or needs that concern or excite you most.

2. If you knew you couldn't fail, and were not afraid, what would you attempt to do for God?

3. Name three dreams you have had in the past or are having presently.

4. If you could have one wish, describe how you would want your world to be.

5. Describe your vision of an ideal relationship with Christ.

1. What is your current vocation?

2. In what other jobs or skills do you have experience?

3. Describe your specialized abilities.

4. What is your most valuable personal asset?

5. What are your three greatest weaknesses?

6. What are your three greatest strengths?

1. Name three important experiences for each decade you have lived.

        Age 0-10
        1.
        2.
        3.

        Age 11-20
        1.
        2.
        3.

        Age 21-30
        1.
        2.
        3.

        Age 31-40
        1.
        2.
        3.

        Age 41-50
        1.
        2.
        3.

        Age 51-60
        1.
        2.
        3.

        Age 61-70
        1.
        2.
        3.

Age 71-80
1.
2.
3.

Age 81 and over
1.
2.
3.

2. Describe your conversion experience.

3. Do a line graph reflecting the ups, downs, and plateaus of your spiritual growth since conversion, making note of corresponding experiences along the way.

4. Describe your personal relationship with Christ today.

Prayer Assignment:

Pray this week for a vision of what God desires for your life.

Considering Your Personality

1. What <u>new</u> thing did you learn about yourself?

2. What did this exercise help you to see about your relationships with others?

3. How does this information impact your view of yourself?

4. What does Christ need to do within your personality for the benefit of the Body of Christ?

5. What steps will you take to accomplish this?

Prayer Assignment:

Pray this week that you will be open to God's making those changes that He sees are needed.

While I feel strongly that every believer's main focus of reading and study should be God's Holy Word, there is a wealth of Christian books that will enrich your faith and give you deeper insights into Biblical truth. I particularly recommend the following books as both a feast for your soul and a light for your path as you continue your journey toward wholeness.

Books by Max Lucado (I love everything he writes, but I especially enjoyed these.)

> *The Great House of God*
> *In the Grip of Grace*
> *When God Whispers Your Name*
> *He Still Moves Stones*
> *No Wonder They Call Him Savior*
> *A Gentle Thunder*

Classic Christianity   by Bob George

Thirty-One Days of Praise by Ruth Myers

The Grace Awakening and *Living Above the Level of Mediocrity* by Charles R. Swindoll

Experiencing God by Henry T. Blackaby & Claude V. King
> (There's a workbook for this that makes it ideal for group study. It was a tremendous blessing for me to do this with women in our church.)

Divine Romance by Gene Edwards
> (This is difficult to read at first. Hang in there!)

Notes from the Illustrator

Few people are given an opportunity of the magnitude that this book has provided me! There are no words to adequately thank Marty for laying the challenge before me of illustrating her book. Designing and producing the book cover alone was overwhelming. Never before have I had to stretch so much while having such a wonderfully good time doing so! I feel certain that I am the book's greatest fan. Marty, your working knowledge of the pitfalls of mankind and Christ's application of His healing in the middle of our tears and brokenness is phenomenal. Your book could certainly stand on its own merits without my illustrations. God bless you, Marty Sholars, for the opportunity you have given me and for your confidence and joyful appreciation of my work.

I must also thank Kay Walter, who is not only a close friend but also one of my biggest fans. Her encouragement and warm compliments fanned my flame! I have never worked with such a gifted writer, and I say this despite all the editorial changes she made in my few attempts to write any of the text. Her deeply grounded faith and never-ending study of God's word made her a perfect match with Marty. What a thrill it has been, Kay. God bless you, too.

What initially seemed an overwhelmingly impossible task became remarkably simplified when I began to pray about each illustration. He "gave" me one set of ideas at a time for the chapters, as Marty and I brainstormed the issues involved. He gave me the people — each for a seemingly good reason — and simply used my hand and my pencils to accomplish them. No one could have been more surprised at the results than I was. What a remarkable experience!

Most of the people represented in these illustrations are friends or relatives — ordinary people who are living, or have lived, extraordinary lives. My illustrations are a way for me to honor these gracious souls. To a person, they walk with Christ. For several, Christ has carried them much of the way.

Chapter 1:   Alicia Yale, my oldest child, wife, mother of three, Registered Nurse, survivor of anorexia/bulimia. Thank you, Lee!

Chapter 2:   Marty's daughter, Meredith, held by Marty's mother, Mrs. Margaret Morphis

Chapter 3:   Nadye Belle Lundy, my widowed mother, who now lives in a nursing home, a victim of Alzheimer's disease. I love you, Mom.
          Dianne Crowley, college friend; lost her only sibling to AIDS. Thank you, Dianne.

Chapter 4:   Christian Schulke, my youngest son, student at Texas A & M. Thank you, Chris.

Chapter 6:   The kneeling figure is one of myself. The hand was modeled by D.B. Lundy, my father's cousin, who lived next door to my home in El Campo, Texas. He died shortly before the book went to press. Despite his life slipping away because of disease, he took a special interest in the book and my drawings for it. His courage in the face of death was evidence of his abiding faith. I miss him very much.

Chapter 7:   Mary Brown, long-time friend of my parents, lives in El Campo. I could think of no one who has "leaned on" Scripture more than she has. Not only was she left alone to raise three young children, her two sons died from complications of hemophilia. Her daughter is a carrier of the disease. Thank you, Mary, for the testimony of your faith in the face of great trials and sorrow.

Chapter 10:   Theresa Webb, neighbor and friend in El Campo, struggled as a single parent of four children following the death of her husband. She fell to the task with great tenacity, devotion, and faith that God would always provide the necessities. Theresa taught me that if you'll just let go of them, God will help solve your problems and bless you many times over. Thank you, Theresa.

Chapter 11: Mark Schulke, my middle child, now a family practice physician living in Oklahoma City, is my favorite doctor! Thank you, Mark.

Chapter 12: Bill and Kathy Robbins of The Woodlands, Texas. It's not easy to draw Jesus Christ. But the moment I saw Bill at a choir rehearsal, I knew I had found the facial qualities that I was looking for. After asking them to let me take some photographs for the drawing I had in mind, I called Marty to say, "I've found Jesus!"   The tear on Christ's cheek was prompted by a sermon given the morning I began my drawing. Dr. Thomas Loftin of El Campo's First United Methodist Church mentioned how moved he was when he saw a painting of Christ with a tear in His eye. Only then did it occur to me that when I am suffering, it saddens Christ as well. Thank you, Bill, Kathy and Tom, for helping me portray what it's like to crawl up into Christ's lap and let Him hold you.

Chapter 14: The cross on the tiny island was drawn from photos taken at Chain-O-Lakes Resort and Conference Center, northeast of Cleveland, Texas. This beautiful, serene setting was the location of a women's retreat in November 1996 sponsored by the Ruth Circle of The Woodlands United Methodist Church. It was here that Kay and I met our retreat speaker, Marty Sholars, for the first time. Little did I realize how much healing, growing, and stretching would follow that weekend encounter.

Chapter 17: For those who are unfamiliar with the term "Spiritus Sanctus," it is Latin for Holy Spirit, which is often symbolized by the dove. Being a Texan, I can imagine how some of you would pronounce it, but, phonetically, it sounds something like this: Spee´-ree-toos Sahnk´-toos. Isn't it wonderful when a beautiful term even sounds beautiful when you say it?

Chapter 18: This illustration is a collage of photos from several dental mission trips to Belize sponsored by The Woodlands United Methodist Church. Any resemblance to any team member is strictly accidental! Actually, the children and the dentist bear a striking resemblance to the actual people. My thanks to Chris Ragan and Kay Walter for providing me with the photos.

Chapter 19: The butterfly is the little fellow I came upon in the parking lot outside Marty's office (see "The Butterfly"), but the hands are those of my brother, Don Lundy. When he came for a short visit, he was quite taken with the book and the illustrations I had completed. I was working on this particular drawing that weekend, and he had an entirely different mental image of Christ's hands, especially the fingers, as He releases the butterfly. We adjourned to the front yard where I shot a number of photographs of his hands releasing an imaginary butterfly. Thank you, Little Brother.

Collage p. 178: Honoring: 1) Marty's parents, Margaret and John Morphis; 2) Kay's mom, Edith Frantz; 3) Nick, Meredith, and Kent Sholars; 4) Mary Brown's sons, Lanier and Byron; and 5) Joy's dad, Rozell Lundy. Collage p. 179: 1) Initial drawing ideas; 2)Joy's son Mark; 3) Chain-O-Lakes; 4) Joy Schulke, Marty Sholars, and Kay Walter.

I cannot close without thanking a loving God without Whom I would have no talent whatsoever. I also would not have come to know Marty and Kay and become involved in this book had there been no personal relationship with Christ. From day one, this book and the illustrations therein have been a "God thing" and such a great joy for me. But the most exciting thing is that He's not through with me yet! Amen and amen.

Joy

Rev. John &
Margaret
Morphis
Edith
Frantz
Rev. Nick
Sholars
Meredith and Kent
Brown
Lanier
1970-1982
Byron 1977-1997
Dad 1916-1996
Rozell
Lundy
1.
2.
3.
4.
5.

SPIRIT
LOVED BY GOD
MIND
RELATIONSHIP W/GOD
VALUE/WORTH
GOD'S PURPOSE FOR US
H
INDI
BOD
SPIRIT
6.
7.
Mark
8.
© 1998 Joy Schulke
Joy
Alice
Joy
Marty
Kay
9.

About the Author

Marty Sholars is a Licensed Professional Counselor, Licensed Marriage and Family Therapist, and Licensed Chemical Dependency Counselor. She is the Director of Providence Clinic of Texas, located in Houston, counseling with individuals, couples, and families experiencing a variety of difficulties.

Marty received her undergraduate degree in psychology and sociology from Texas Wesleyan College and a Master's degree in counseling from Stephen F. Austin State University. Before joining Providence Clinic, she was the Director of the Minirth Meier Clinic in Houston, Texas. She has worked with adolescents and adults in both inpatient and outpatient settings.

The daughter of a United Methodist minister, Marty's approach to counseling is an expression of her confidence in Christ as the Great Healer. She feels strongly that, apart from Christ, healing is only partial at best and that His involvement is essential to bring healing to the whole person — spirit, mind, emotions, and body.

Marty and her husband, who is also a United Methodist minister, have been married for more than 20 years. They have two children. In her leisure time, Marty enjoys jogging, swimming, and hiking.